Sophocles

Oedipus Tyrannus

A new translation and
commentary by Ian McAuslan
and Judith Affleck

Introduction to the Greek Theatre
by P.E. Easterling

Series Editors: John Harrison and Judith Affleck

THE LEARNING CENTRE
HAMMERSMITH AND WEST
LONDON COLLEGE
GLIDDON ROAD
LONDON W14 9BL

HAMMERSMITH WEST LONDON COLLEGE

330787

CAMBRIDGE UNIVERSITY PRESS
Cambridge, New York, Melbourne, Madrid, Cape Town,
Singapore, São Paulo, Delhi, Tokyo, Mexico City

Cambridge University Press
The Edinburgh Building, Cambridge CB2 8RU, UK

www.cambridge.org
Information on this title: www.cambridge.org/9780521010726

First published 2003
9th printing 2011

Printed in the United Kingdom at the University Press, Cambridge

A catalogue record for this publication is available from the British Library

ISBN 978-0-521-01072-6 Paperback

ACKNOWLEDGEMENTS
Thanks are due to the following for permission to reproduce photographs:
p. 3, Reproduced courtesy of the Trustees of the Victoria and Albert Museum;
p. 5, The Mansell Collection; p. 11, McKague, Toronto; p. 33, Copyright BBC
Photo Library; p. 37, Donald Cooper/Photostage; p. 56, bfi Collections; pp.
61, 98, John Vickers; p. 65, © Robbie Jack/CORBIS; p. 84, Bibliothèque
Nationale, Paris.

Every effort has been made to reach copyright holders. The publishers would
be glad to hear from anyone whose right they have unknowingly infringed.

Maps on p. vii by Helen Humphreys and Peter Simmonett.
Cover picture: Detail from Oedipus and the Sphinx (1808) by Jean Auguste
Dominique Ingres, courtesy of the Louvre/Bridgeman Art Library.

PERFORMANCE
For permission to give a public performance of this translation of *Oedipus
Tyrannus* please write to Permissions Department, Cambridge University Press
The Edinburgh Building, Shaftesbury Road, Cambridge CB2 8RU.

Contents

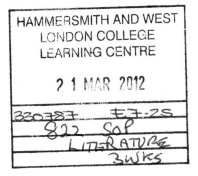

Preface

The aim of the series is to enable students to approach Classical plays with confidence and understanding: to discover the play within the text.

The translations are new. Many recent versions of Greek tragedy have been produced by poets and playwrights who do not work from the original Greek. The translators of this series aim to bring readers, actors and directors as close as possible to the playwrights' actual words and intentions: to create translations which are faithful to the original in content and tone; and which are speakable, with all the immediacy of modern English.

The notes are designed for students of Classical Civilisation and Drama, and indeed anyone who is interested in theatre. They address points which present difficulty to the reader of today: chiefly relating to the Greeks' religious and moral attitudes, their social and political life, and mythology.

Our hope is that students should discover the play for themselves. The conventions of the Classical theatre are discussed, but there is no thought of recommending 'authentic' performances. Different groups will find different ways of responding to each play. The best way of bringing alive an ancient play, as any other, is to explore the text practically, to stimulate thought about ways of staging the plays today. Stage directions in the text are minimal, and the notes are not prescriptive; rather, they contain questions and exercises which explore the dramatic qualities of the text. Bullet points introduce suggestions for discussion and analysis; open bullet points focus on more practical exercises.

If the series encourages students to attempt a staged production, so much the better. But the primary aim is understanding and enjoyment.

This translation of *Oedipus Tyrannus* is based on the the Greek text, edited by H. Lloyd-Jones and N. G. Wilson for Oxford University Press. The line numbers in this translation correspond with those in the Greek text; occasionally in the lyric passages the number of lines has been condensed or expanded. All translations from Homer's *Odyssey* are from the Penguin translation, revised by Christopher Rieu and Peter Jones.

John Harrison
Judith Affleck

Background to the story of Oedipus Tyrannus

(*The names of characters who appear in this play are printed in* **bold**.)

Most if not all members of Sophocles' original audience would have known three things about **Oedipus**: that he had defeated a female monster called the Sphinx and had thus come to rule the city of Thebes, that he had unwittingly killed his own father, and that he had equally unwittingly married his own mother. As was the way with Greek myths, at different times and in different places the story was told and represented in different ways: some members of the original audience may have seen paintings on walls and on pots showing Oedipus confronting the Sphinx (painters seem to have concentrated on this aspect of the story – see page 6 and illustration on page 5); others may have studied in school or heard professional reciters performing that part of the *Odyssey* (book *xi*) in which Odysseus visits the House of the Dead, meets the ghost of the Theban seer **Tiresias**, who tells him about trials that he has yet to undergo, and sees the ghost of Oedipus' mother, who has hanged herself when 'the gods made these things [i.e. the patricide and incest] known among men'. The poet of the *Odyssey* calls Oedipus' mother Epikaste; Sophocles calls her **Jocasta** – an example of the variation common to the telling of such stories. Others still may just have heard the stories told to them at home when they were children. Many will have seen earlier plays on the same theme.

Sophocles' elder contemporary Aeschylus had written a trilogy of tragedies on the story of Oedipus – *Laius, Oedipus* and *Seven against Thebes* – of which only the last survives. As with his more famous trilogy, the *Oresteia*, he seems to have shown the working out of a family curse (see notes on 417 and 1246–7 and *Genealogical table,* page viii). The Theban king Laius, son of Labdacus, had seduced the son of Pelops, king of Argos, and Pelops had cursed him. Laius had married Jocasta, sister of **Creon** and daughter of Menoeceus, but they had failed to produce children. He therefore consulted the oracle of Apollo at Delphi and was warned that if he and Jocasta produced a son, that son would kill him. In due course, Oedipus was born, was exposed to die, but survived and later (in ignorance) killed his father and married his mother. When he discovered what he had done, he in turn cursed Eteocles and Polynices, the sons whom he had incestuously sired on Jocasta, and in the final play of the trilogy the curse was worked out when the brothers fought over their inheritance and killed one another in single combat.

Sophocles' play focuses on Oedipus' act of discovery and its consequences. Most of the story emerges during the course of the action, and all that Sophocles really wants his audience to bear in mind at the outset as they watch Oedipus is the three things mentioned above – the defeat of the Sphinx which made Oedipus king of Thebes, the patricide, and the incest. The defeat of the Sphinx had consisted in the answering of a riddle, which exists in various versions, but which runs something like this:

> There is on earth a being with two feet, four feet and three feet, but with only one name; it alone, of all creatures that move on earth, in the sky or in the sea, changes its form. The more feet it has, the more feeble and slow its movement. (See page 6.)

Sophocles also makes much of the various messages issuing from the oracle of Apollo at Delphi; like the Sphinx's riddle, they are paradoxical, involved and enigmatic, and they need intelligence to interpret them. The theme of human intelligence and its limits lies at the root of this play.

The action is set in Thebes, an independent city-state about seventy kilometres north of Sophocles' Athens. At the time of the play's production the two cities were on opposite sides in an extended war.

Suggestions for further reading

Felix Budelmann, 'Oedipus' ongoing tragedy', *OMNIBUS*, 39 (2000), pp. 20–3

Michael Comber, 'Suspense and Sensibility: Sophocles' *Oedipus the King*', *OMNIBUS*, 32 (1996), pp. 11–13

E.R. Dodds, 'On Misunderstanding the *Oedipus Rex*', in Erich Segal (ed.) *Oxford Readings in Greek Tragedy*, Oxford University Press, 1983, pp. 177–88

B.M.W. Knox, *Oedipus at Thebes: Sophocles' Tragic Hero and his Time*, 2nd edition, New Haven and London, Yale University Press, 1998

Charles Segal, *Oedipus Tyrannus: Tragic Heroism and the Limits of Knowledge*, 2nd edition, Oxford University Press, 2000

Jean-Pierre Vernant, 'Oedipus without the Complex', in Jean-Pierre Vernant and Pierre Vidal-Naquet, *Myth and Tragedy in Ancient Greece*, New York, Zone Books, 1990, pp. 85–111

Map of Ancient Greece

Genealogical table

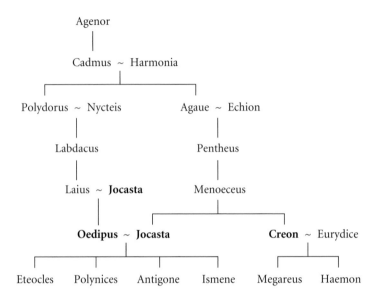

List of characters

(Non-speaking parts are marked with an asterisk.)

OEDIPUS	king of Thebes
CROWD OF SUPPLIANTS*	citizens of Thebes
PRIEST	a priest of Zeus
CREON	brother-in-law of Oedipus
CHORUS	elders of Thebes
TIRESIAS	a blind seer
JOCASTA	wife of Oedipus and sister of Creon
FIRST MESSENGER	a former herdsman from Corinth
SERVANT	a herdsman and former servant of Laius and Jocasta
SECOND MESSENGER	a palace servant
ANTIGONE AND ISMENE*	daughters of Oedipus and Jocasta

PROLOGUE (1–150)

The opening scene depicts a civic gathering: a deputation of citizens is grouped before the king of Thebes. In the original production the *skēnē* (stage building, see page 114) would have represented the royal palace. In front of the palace are altars (16), one of which is sacred to Lycean Apollo (919).

- What other incidental details of the scene and of the people assembled can be gathered from lines 1–21?
- In a modern indoor production the lights might come up revealing a 'tableau'. In the original open-air production all the characters would be visible as they entered the *orchēstra* (see page 114*).* Consider different ways of staging the opening.

Sophoclean prologues

The term for the opening scene of a Greek tragedy prior to the arrival of the Chorus (see 151) is the *prologue*. In it often a single character sets the events of the play in context. In his seven surviving plays Sophocles differs from Euripides and Aeschylus in preferring to open the action with more than one character in dialogue.

1 Children The people Oedipus addresses include old men as well as children (9, 16–17). His first word in the play suggests paternal benevolence (see 58, note on 96, 142; also (the priest speaking) 147).

1 new blood of old Cadmus Cadmus was the founder of Thebes. The Delphic oracle commanded him to found a city in Boeotia, sowing a dragon's teeth to create a new earth-born population whose descendants are addressed here. (See *Genealogical table*, page viii; 29.)

3 supplication In ancient Greece, the weak might 'supplicate' those with power: for example, a defeated enemy would beg for mercy. Suppliants were seen as being under the protection of Zeus, most powerful god of all. Supplication usually involved kneeling and touching the chin or knee of the person whose favour was being sought. Here the people of Thebes are kneeling and carry ritual emblems of supplication – branches of olive or laurel draped with wool. Supplication by mortals of gods generally took the form of prayer (see 913, 920).

5 the Healer One of the titles of the god Apollo (see note on 154).

8 'Famous Oedipus' Oedipus' reference to his past has a heroic ring and reminds the audience that there is a story behind his rise to kingship. Further hints or reminders are dropped in the course of the Prologue (35–57). To the original audience, the story of Oedipus and the Sphinx was well known (see *Background to the story*, page v).

OEDIPUS Children, new blood of old Cadmus,
　　　　Why are you all sitting here before me,
　　　　Carrying branches of supplication?
　　　　The city is full of the smell of incense,
　　　　Of hymns to the Healer and cries of suffering.　　　　　　5
　　　　I thought it wrong to rely on the reports
　　　　Of others, so have come here myself,
　　　　'Famous Oedipus', as everyone calls me.
　　　　Old man, tell me – it is right that you
　　　　Should speak for these people – what has brought you all here?　10
　　　　Fear, or some request? I am ready
　　　　To give any help I can. I would be a hard man
　　　　Not to feel sympathy for a gathering like this.

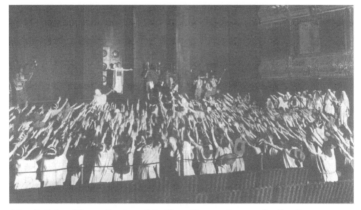

Max Reinhardt's production of Oedipus Rex *at Covent Garden in 1912.*

Priests and gods

Ancient Greece was a polytheistic society and the people of Thebes appeal to several different gods for help (see note on 21). The old man selected by Oedipus to be the people's spokesman is a priest of Zeus. Priests were concerned principally with ritual: maintaining the temple, receiving offerings and presiding at sacrifices. They might help lead civic prayers but did not monopolise religious actions or decisions. The distinction between religion and government was slight; city authorities were involved in the management of religion.

14 ruler of my country (See note on 35.)

16 Sitting at your altars These words contrast with those of Oedipus, 'sitting here before me' (2). Although there is no necessary conflict in supplicating both man and god, the priest emphasises the religious nature of his appeal. There is an ambiguity in the words 'your altars'; the priest, however, is careful not to confuse Oedipus with a god (31).

20–1 at the twin shrines/Of Athene Athene was the protecting goddess of Athens, but was worshipped all over the Greek world. It would not be unusual to have more than one temple devoted to a single god (e.g. in Athens the temples of Athene Parthenos and Athene Nike are near to each other on Athens' citadel, the Acropolis).

21 the prophetic embers of Ismenus Ismenus was a local river that had close links with Apollo. Here the reference is to an oracular altar in Thebes. The embers show that the fire is *dying* because divination (consultation of the gods by burnt offerings) has already been tried.

The priest's language

The priest's language is colourful, rich in metaphor. He likens the youngest members of the gathering to baby birds, barely able to fly (16–17), and uses the repeated image of agricultural blight in 'wasting' (25–6). See also notes on 27, 30 and 39. He introduces the simile of the city as a ship and Oedipus as its helmsman (23–4, note on 56), an image used by others later in the play (104, 423, 923).

● What other aspects of the priest's language are striking?

27 The fiery god (plague) is later identified with Ares (see 190).

29 the house of Cadmus is the city of Thebes (see note on 1).

30 black Hades Hades was god of the underworld, the destination of the dead. Hades is growing rich (*ploutizetai*) from those dying in the plague. The priest makes a grim pun on his alternative name, Plouton (Pluto in Latin), linked with the word for wealth or riches (*ploutos*).

PRIEST Oedipus, ruler of my country,
You see us here – people of all ages   15
Sitting at your altars, some not yet
Strong enough to have flown far, others bowed with age;
Priests – I serve Zeus – and the pick of our young men.
The rest of the people, holding suppliant branches,
Are sitting in the town squares, at the twin shrines   20
Of Athene, and by the prophetic embers of Ismenus.
The city, as you can see for yourself,
Is like a ship caught in a storm at sea, unable
To keep afloat and escape the deadly waves.
She's wasting away – in the husks her soil produces,   25
Wasting away in the pasturing herds, and in the children
Stillborn to our women. The fiery god has struck
And is driving our city – a plague hated by all.
He is emptying the house of Cadmus; and with our groans
And lamentations, black Hades is growing rich.   30

Interior of Attic red-figure cup by the Oedipus Painter.
Oedipus and the Sphinx.

Blight

The priest graphically reveals the nature of the crisis: the city is stricken by a blight that prevents new growth and is destroying it.

31 It is not because we think of you as the gods' equal Failing to recognise the distinction between god and man was believed by the Greeks to lead to terrible consequences.

35 It was you, when you came to this city We learn here that Oedipus has not always lived in Thebes (hence, perhaps, the priest's address in 14 as 'ruler of *my* country') and that he has saved them in the past by solving the Sphinx's riddle.

The riddle of the Sphinx

'The remorseless singer' (36) is a reference to the well-known story of the Sphinx (see note on 8). She is named at 130 (compare 391, 507) (see illustration on page 5). The Theban Sphinx set a riddle and 'bound' (*sphinxai*) the Thebans to answer it. The riddle itself is never quoted in Sophocles' *Oedipus* but other versions survive (see *Background to the story*, page vi). As will be seen, the thematic significance of the riddle to the play is all-pervasive. (See **One witness, one clue** page 12.)

39 you set our lives to rights The idea of setting straight or upright (Greek: *orth-*) recurs in the priest's appeal (see 46, 50, 51). The image may suggest the raising of a suppliant or keeping a ship or chariot on course.

40 all-powerful ruler 46 best of men
● Does the priest flatter Oedipus?

43 knowledge from either god or man The priest speculates on how Oedipus was able to solve the riddle when others had failed. He speaks of Oedipus' 'readiness to act' (48) and seems to accept the possibility of some sort of divine assistance (38, 52). Later Oedipus expresses his own view on the source of his knowledge (398).

56 A walled town, like a ship This metaphor recurs, as do sea-faring metaphors generally (see **The priest's language** page 4).

Oedipus and the priest
● Both Oedipus and the priest are figures of authority: from where does each derive that authority? What relationship has been established between them in lines 1–57?
● How do you account for the warning tone of lines 46–57?

It is not because we think of you as the gods' equal
That I and these boys are sitting as your suppliants.
We judge that you more than any man can guide us
In life's troubles and in dealings with the gods.
It was you, when you came to this city, who delivered us   35
From the toll that we paid to the remorseless singer.
You did this without any special knowledge
Or instruction from us; it was with some god's help,
So men say and believe, that you set our lives to rights.
Now, Oedipus, all-powerful ruler,   40
All of us here turn to you in supplication
To find us some help – perhaps some message you have heard,
Giving you knowledge from either god or man.
As I see it, it is those with experience
Whose advice most often leads to effective action.   45
Come then, best of men, raise up our city –
Come, but take care: this land now calls you 'saviour'
Because of your readiness to act before.
Never let us remember your reign
As one that set us upright, only to let us fall.   50
Hold this city up, and keep her safe.
A bird of good omen was with you when you helped us before.
Bring us that same luck now.
If you're to go on ruling this land as now you do,
Better to rule men than a desert.   55
A walled town, like a ship, is worth nothing
If it is empty, with no one to man it.

58–9 I know … I fully understand … I am well aware Oedipus speaks emphatically of his understanding. His last verb of knowing (*oida* in Greek) suggests his own name, *Oidi-pous* (*pous* in Greek means foot) (see also notes on 397, 1036). Man's knowledge – and its limitations – is the dominant theme in this play.

- What other signs of mental activity does Oedipus give in his speech (58–77)?

Sickness

Oedipus uses the city's sufferings as a metaphor for his own situation. He develops an argument about the relationship between ruler and ruled in which he as ruler comes to represent the city collectively, channelling its cares. Elsewhere he again claims that his individual interests are subordinate to those of the state (93–4, 443; 1411).

68 only one remedy Sustaining the metaphor, Oedipus prescribes as cure the consultation of the oracle at Delphi. The idea of treating the blight on the city as something requiring medical or human healing is not entertained: as in Homer's *Iliad i*, the problem is recognised as being of divine origin (see note on 154 and **Plague?** page 16).

70 Creon, my own brother-in-law See *Genealogical table*, page viii. Oedipus' marriage is first alluded to here (see 260).

The Delphic oracle

The oracle of Apollo in Delphi, on the slopes of Mt Parnassus (see 475, map on page vii), had been the most famous in the Greek world for the best part of three hundred years when this play was written. For states and individuals to travel to Delphi (the 'earth's navel' 481) to consult the oracle was regular practice in the late fifth century when this play was first produced. The advice given was often obscure or ambiguous. In this play three crucial oracles from Delphi are rejected or not understood by their human recipients.

Oedipus the king (see note on 514)

- What impressions of Oedipus as ruler have you formed from the opening 77 lines of the play?
- How might these impressions affect the way in which Oedipus might be dressed and move in a modern performance? Would he wear the trappings of royal power (see, for example, the picture on page 11)? How might this contrast with the priest's costume? Should Oedipus mingle amongst his people or keep his distance?

OEDIPUS I know, poor children, I fully understand
    The desire that has brought you here; I am well aware
    Of your sickness. But the sickness that you all suffer   60
    Is less than mine – none of you can match it.
    The pain you feel is a private one –
    Your own, no one else's; whereas I groan in my heart
    For the city, for myself, and for each one of you.
    You are not stirring me out of some deep slumber;   65
    Believe me, I've shed many tears
    And let my mind range over many paths of thought.
    After careful reflection I could find only one remedy:
    This I've pursued. I have sent the son of Menoeceus,
    Creon, my own brother-in-law, to Apollo's shrine   70
    In Delphi, to see if he can find out
    What I can say or do to save this city.
    In fact, I have been counting off the days
    And I'm worried; he has been away for longer
    Than expected – longer than he should be taking.   75
    But when he does come, then I would be wrong
    Not to do all that the god makes clear.
PRIEST Your remark is well timed; these people have just now
    Pointed out to me Creon approaching.

The arrival of Creon

Oedipus' words expressing anxiety about Creon's late return (73–5) anticipate his arrival on stage. The size of Greek theatres contributed to the audience's difficulty in recognising new characters and it was conventional to identify them as they arrived. In the original production Creon would have appeared from one of the *parodoi* (see plan of the Greek theatre, page 114).

83 thickly crowned with laurel The priest is first to spot the wreath of laurel, sacred to the god Apollo.

87 Good news Creon's next words hint that the 'cure' will not be easy.

92 perhaps you'd rather go inside In Greek tragedy there is a practical problem about reporting 'private words' (which could not be heard if they were spoken 'inside' the *skēnē*), but Sophocles seems deliberately to highlight this moment of decision, indicating a possible alternative to the public proclamation that follows.

● What differences in their characters/views on government do Creon's remark and Oedipus' reply at lines 91–4 suggest?

Pollution (*miasma*)

The idea that a community could be infected by the impious act of an individual ran deep in ancient Greek thought. Often murderers had to leave their community and travel to find purification. The best-known case in the Greek tragic world was that of Orestes, whose search for purification for the murder of his mother forms the subject of the *Eumenides*, the concluding play of Aeschylus' trilogy the *Oresteia* (see note on 472, line 1012). The historian Thucydides describes an attempt to use a blood-curse to exile Pericles, the pre-eminent politician of his day, not long before this play is thought to have been written (i. 126–7).

Clear instructions?

In lines 96–111 Creon gradually reveals what the oracle has said, twice stating that these instructions are clear (97, 106). Oracular responses are typically obscure (see note on **The Delphic oracle**, page 8, and on 791–3) and it would be unlikely, for example, that Laius was named as the murder victim (103).

● How clear are the words of the oracle? Do you think Creon is quoting or paraphrasing? Does it matter (see 243, 306–9)?

96 The pollution we've been nursing The Greek word (*treph-/troph-*) occurs frequently in this play. It means to rear, feed or nurture and is used in the first line of the 'new blood' (more literally 'new brood/rearing') of Cadmus. (See also 98, 323, 374 'wrapped'.)

OEDIPUS Lord Apollo, may he bring salvation,   80
  As the brightness in his eye suggests he does.
PRIEST I would guess his news is welcome – otherwise
  His head wouldn't be so thickly crowned with laurel.
OEDIPUS We'll know soon enough; he's within hearing distance.
  My lord, son of Menoeceus, brother,   85
  What message do you bring us from the god?
CREON Good news. For I say that even hardship
  Is all for the best, if the outcome is good.
OEDIPUS But what did the oracle say? Your words just now
  Can give me neither confidence nor fear.   90
CREON If you want to hear me with all these people near
  I'm ready to speak; but perhaps you'd rather go inside.
OEDIPUS Speak out in front of us all. I suffer more
  For these people than for myself.
CREON I'll tell you what I heard from the god.   95
  The pollution we've been nursing in this land –
  Apollo clearly orders us, my lord,
  To drive it out, not nurture it; it can't be cured.

*Douglas Campbell as Oedipus in the Stratford (Ontario) Festival's
production of* Oedipus Rex, *directed by Tyrone Guthrie, 1955.*

103 Laius King of Thebes and husband of Queen Jocasta before Oedipus (see *Genealogical table*, page viii).

104 set the city back on course This image is to do with steering in the right direction, developing the nautical idea of the city as a ship and Oedipus as helmsman (see notes on 39 and 56).

109 Any trail will be hard to find Oedipus uses hunting imagery (see 221, 476 and note on 541).

112 Was Laius murdered at home or in the country? Oedipus' speech since the arrival of Creon has been largely a sequence of questions. Now, with characteristic *prothūmia* ('readiness to act' 48), he launches his 'search' in obedience to the oracle's instructions (see note on 278). The effect of these questions is to inform not only Oedipus but also the audience of the recent history of Thebes before the Sphinx's reign of terror and Oedipus' victory (see note on 8).

114 He'd left Thebes – to consult the oracle We do not hear what Laius' intended question to the oracle was. In Euripides' *Phoenissae* (see **Sophoclean prologues** page 2) his childlessness is given as a reason – a common enough motive (Aegeus in Euripides' *Medea* asks oracular advice on the same question) but one which, for reasons which become apparent, does not suit Sophocles' version.

One witness, one clue

Despite – or perhaps because of – Oedipus' eager questioning, he appears not to master the one clue offered to him. Oedipus is told of a witness (118–19), a fact he does not follow up until line 765; he is also told – emphatically – that Laius was the victim of a group of robbers (122–3), yet in the next line Oedipus uses the singular (see also 247; cf. 845). This is perhaps surprising for a man who has shown awareness of the importance of number (e.g. his counting off the days of Creon's absence (73–5) and his solution of the Sphinx's riddle – see **The riddle of the Sphinx** page 6).

● Suggest reasons for Oedipus' use of the singular in line 124.

125 Unless he was hired to do the job by someone here? This is the germ of a conspiracy theory that Oedipus will develop in the following scene (see 378–403).

128 What 'trouble' stopped you…? Oedipus' question carries with it a reproach, understandable coming from the ruler who had taken the dead king's place (see also 138–41). He repeats the question to Creon later in the play (566).

● How excusable do you find Creon's response to this criticism? Whose responsibility was it to carry out an investigation?

OEDIPUS How can we cleanse ourselves? How have things gone
     so wrong?

CREON Someone must be exiled, or a death must pay for a death.   100
    The spilling of blood has brought this storm on the city.

OEDIPUS Who is the man? Whose fate does the god refer to?

CREON My lord, Laius was once the ruler of this land –
    Before you set the city back on course.

OEDIPUS I know – I've heard of him, though I never saw him.   105

CREON He was killed, and now our instructions are clear:
    To make those who killed him pay.

OEDIPUS Where are these men? The crime happened long ago;
    Any trail will be hard to find. Where do we start?

CREON In this land, he said. If we search, we can find it;   110
    But if we're negligent, it slips our grasp.

OEDIPUS Was Laius murdered at home or in the country?
    Or did he meet his death in some other land?

CREON He'd left Thebes – to consult the oracle, he said.
    But after he'd gone he never came home again.   115

OEDIPUS Was there no messenger, no fellow traveller who saw
    What happened – someone from whom we could usefully learn?

CREON Dead, all but one. He fled in fear and couldn't talk
    Clearly about what he saw – except for one thing.

OEDIPUS What was that? We could learn a lot from one clue.   120
    Even a small start might give us grounds for hope.

CREON He said it was a group of robbers who met Laius
    And killed him – working together, not just one man.

OEDIPUS What could have made a robber so daring –
    Unless he was hired to do the job by someone here?   125

CREON This was suspected; but after Laius died,
    We had our troubles, and no one to help us.

OEDIPUS What 'trouble' stopped you from learning all there was
     to know,
    When your ruler had died in such circumstances?

131 Immediate problems The Greek literally says 'what was at our feet'.

A fresh start

Oedipus is plausibly portrayed as an energetic leader, full of confidence and resolution. The contrast with the same man at the end of the play will be stark. He does not anticipate how far back he will need to go to find 'the beginning'.

137–8 it's not for some distant friend/But for my own sake In Athenian law prosecutions for murder could only be initiated by a relative of the victim. Oedipus' insistence on his connection with Laius (see also 258–64; cf. note on 128) seems in part a justification for taking up the 'case'. Those familiar with the myth of Oedipus (see *Background to the story*, page v) will recognise the chilling irony in these words (see **Dramatic irony** page 22).

142 Quick as you can now, children, rise from these steps A sense of closure is given to the opening scene by these words which echo the first lines of the play.

144 Someone, go and bring the people of Cadmus together here Oedipus' words herald the arrival of the Chorus. We heard from the priest that throughout Thebes prayers and offerings are being made at the city's shrines (19–21). As the Chorus – consisting of citizens of Thebes (see page 16) – enter the *orchēstra* singing, the audience hear their prayers.

147–8 This man has publicly/Proclaimed all that we came for The priest closes with a prayer to Apollo and leaves with his group of suppliants. It remains to be seen how Apollo will answer.

● Is the priest right to be satisfied with Oedipus' response?

Review of the Prologue

● What have we learned of Oedipus' character and background from his own words and the priest's response to him?
○ Consider the physical appearance of the suppliants. How might they be dressed? Would it be more effective if they remain still during the scene, or move about? How mobile should they be? What effects are created by increasing or decreasing the numbers in the deputation? (See the picture on page 3.)

CREON The Sphinx, with her riddling songs, made us look to   130
    Immediate problems, putting aside unsolved mysteries.

OEDIPUS Then I shall go back to the beginning again, and make
      all clear.

    Apollo has done well, and so have you,
    To draw attention to the dead man's cause.
    You will, then, find in me a true ally –   135
    Seeking vengeance for this land, and for the god as well.
    After all, it's not for some distant friend
    But for my own sake that I'll be ridding us of this pollution.
    For whoever it was that killed Laius
    May choose to strike again, just as violently,   140
    So in assisting him, I am helping myself.
    Quick as you can now, children, rise from these steps
    And take away your branches of supplication.
    Someone, go and bring the people of Cadmus together here
    To witness that I will do all I can: either, with the god's help,   145
    We shall be seen to prosper – or to fall.

PRIEST Let us rise now, children. This man has publicly
    Proclaimed all that we came for.
    May Apollo, who sent this oracle,
    Come to save and deliver us from our plague.   150

PARODOS (ENTRY OF THE CHORUS) (151–215)

The chorus was central to Athenian tragedy; it may have developed out of choral songs and dances in honour of Dionysus. Once the chorus have entered they remain until the end – observing and commenting on the action. All odes are in lyric metres and were sung; most are arranged in pairs of stanzas (*strophē* and *antistrophē*) where the second mirrors the rhythms (and probably the dance steps) of the first. The language tends to be rich and rhythmically complex. The Chorus in this play consists of 'elders' (1110).

News of the oracle's response has passed swiftly through the city. The Chorus speculate about it (151–7), then begin a prayer of supplication (158–67). A lament follows, developing some of the priest's images of plague. This ends with further appeals to Apollo and Athene (168–89). In 190–202 the Chorus launch an attack on Ares as god of destruction, calling on Zeus as champion. Finally they rally Apollo, Artemis and Dionysus to oppose Ares (203–15).

151 Sweet voice of Zeus, in what guise have you come From at least the time of Homer's *Iliad* human destiny was represented as dependent on Zeus' will. The prophecy from Zeus' son Apollo could not come without his sanction and the two generally work in harmony (see note on 469–70). The Chorus seem not to know the nature of the prophecy, merely that the oracle has responded (see First *Stasimon* page 38).

154 Delian lord of healing The reference here and in 162 is to Apollo, who with his twin sister Artemis (159, 207) was born on Delos. Most of Apollo's attributes are benevolent: he is god of healing, the sun, music and the arts, and prophecy. But much in Greek thought is viewed in terms of opposites: as god of healing he is also the god who can bring plague. The Chorus show both mortal dread and hope. Apollo is the most pervasive divine presence in the play; in the *Parodos* he is invoked again at lines 162 and 203–5; his 'unerring arrows' are used in *Iliad i* against the Greeks at Troy (see note on 68 and **Pollution** page 10).

158 Athene (See note on 20–1.)

159 Artemis (See note on 154.) Twin of Apollo, daughter of Zeus and Leto (worshipped as goddess 'of Fair Repute').

Plague?

Some of the details in lines 174–85 suggest the blight is not only affecting those yet to be born. In Sophocles' lifetime Athens experienced plague as a result of overcrowding in 429–425 BC, the early years of the Peloponnesian War documented in Thucydides *ii*. The date of *Oedipus Tyrannus* is uncertain but it may belong to this period.

CHORUS Sweet voice of Zeus, in what guise have you come
From golden Delphi to glorious Thebes?
I am tense with fear; my heart shakes in dread of you,
Delian lord of healing,
What debt will you be calling in –   155
A new one or an old – as the seasons come round?
Tell me, child of golden Hope, immortal Oracle.
First I call on you, daughter of Zeus, deathless Athene,
Then on sister Artemis,
Famed guardian of our land,   160
Seated on her throne in the heart of our city;
Thirdly I ask Phoebus the archer:
Trinity of gods, appear before us, protecting us from death.
When ruin loomed
Over our city before   165
You banished its searing flame,
So come to us again now.

Ah, I have lost count of my sufferings.
All the people of my city are sick,
And there is no weapon we can think of   170
To defend ourselves. Nothing grows
From our rich soil; our women have no live births
To help them through the cries of labour.
One after another you can see the dead,
Like birds of omen,   175
Speeding more fiercely than unquenchable fire
To the coast of the god of darkness.

And, losing count of its dead,
The city dies.
Its children lie unpitied and unlamented   180
On the ground, infected with death;
Meanwhile, wives and white-haired mothers
Come from all over the city to the altar-ground,
Crying for deliverance
From the suffering that destroys them.   185

Lament

Lines 168–87 consist of a lament for the city. The repetition 'lost/losing count' (168 and 178) helps bind together these two stanzas.

● How closely do the details correspond with those given by the priest in 25–30? How do the two descriptions differ in language and intensity?

○ In the original production, the *Parodos* would have been sung. Consider what effects might be achieved by adding a simple rhythmical accompaniment to these lines.

190 Ares The representation of Ares almost as the personification of destruction is striking as we see the desperate and impassioned response of the Thebans to their relentless suffering. Thucydides (*ii*, ch. 49) records the sensation of burning (see also 27) in his account of the symptoms of the plague in Athens (see **Plague?** page 16). The Chorus' wish that Ares should be routed or 'Wafted by the winds' (195) is a poetic expression of their desire for his destructive violence to end.

195–6 to Amphitrite's great bedchamber/Or to the Thracian breakers Thrace was to the far north-east of Greece. The bedchamber of Amphitrite, wife of the sea-god Poseidon, is likely to be the Atlantic.

209 Bacchus is an alternative name for Dionysus, the god within whose sacred precinct in Athens the theatre stood. The Chorus' appeal is particularly appropriate since by tradition Dionysus was born in Thebes. His associations with wine, Bacchants (his ecstatic female followers with their characteristic cry, *Euhoe!* 211–12) and the riches of the East ('gold-turbaned' 209), where Dionysus reputedly travelled before returning to establish his worship in Greece, are alluded to here (see also 1105).

Review of the *Parodos*

● How do the invocations of gods in the last two stanzas differ from those in the first two? How different is the tone?

● Is there any sense from the Chorus that Apollo is responsible for the blight?

○ What sort of effects could be produced by use of either separate voices or instruments to characterise the different gods and ideas in this ode?

The prayer to the Healer blazes out
In unison with the voice of suffering.
Answer them, golden daughter of Zeus:
Send your sweet-faced protection.

As for Ares, the destroyer,   190
Who, without armour of bronze,
Now faces me in the fray surrounded by screams,
And burns me up,
Make him turn tail and rush in flight from my land,
Wafted by the winds to Amphitrite's great bedchamber   195
Or to the Thracian breakers
Hostile to ships;
For if night offers any relief,
He comes by day to complete his work.
Father Zeus, you control the fiery lightning: 200
Blast Ares to a cinder
With your thunderbolt.

Apollo, lord of light,
May your arrows be our aid and our defence –
Shot unerringly from your gold-strung bow –   205
And those fiery torches
With which Artemis speeds
Through the mountains of Lycia;
I call upon Bacchus too, gold-turbaned,
God of this land   210
Flushed with wine, summoned with a cry
By his own troop of ecstatic women:
Come close, blazing
With radiant pine-brand
Against Ares, a god dishonoured among gods.   215

FIRST EPISODE (216–462)
Stage directions
Most entrances and exits are indicated by the actors or chorus (see **The arrival of Creon** page 10). We are not told whether Oedipus remains on stage during the *Parodos*.

○ What are the dramatic advantages and disadvantages of Oedipus remaining visible for part or all of the *Parodos*?

216–18 You pray… Oedipus seems confident that the answer to his people's prayers lies in human action and enquiry.

● How 'godlike' does Oedipus sound in his opening words here? (cf. 31–43)

○ Compare the tone of the opening words of the play and lines 58–67 with Oedipus' lines here. How might an actor or director reflect any change (voice, costume, attendants etc.)?

219 a stranger Oedipus draws attention to the difference between his own history as a newcomer and that of the Thebans, suggesting (ironically, as it turns out – see **Dramatic irony** page 22) that he is in the weakest position to find the killer.

221 some clue The Greek word for 'clue' is *sumbolon*, a sign or token (see note on 1059). Oedipus seems to suggest that he is already 'on the trail' (see note on 109). As well as establishing that Laius was murdered, he has had some preliminary thoughts as to motive (see 124–5), including the hypothesis that the murderer may strike again (140).

Oedipus' proclamation
Consider lines 224–43 of Oedipus' proclamation.

● Public appeals on radio or television to help catch a criminal are familiar to us. How does Oedipus' approach here compare with these?

● What qualities in Oedipus as a ruler are revealed? Among others, consider the following adjectives: *merciful, resolute, weak, ruthless, tyrannical, kind, practical, optimistic.*

○ Where might an actor pause during these lines and for what effect? How might the Chorus respond?

230–1 a stranger/From abroad See **Dramatic irony** page 22, note on 350–1 and 452.

The consequences
Refusing an individual the communal privileges mentioned in lines 237–40 in effect means exclusion and disgrace. The heaviness of this penalty is a recurrent subject in the heroic world of Greek tragedy. In the fifth century, too, exile was a powerful form of degradation (see Herodotus *viii*, ch. 61; Thucydides *i*, ch. 126–7).

OEDIPUS You pray. Now in answer to your prayers, if you are willing
    To hear and accept my words and attend to this sickness,
    You will find protection and relief from your afflictions.
    I shall be speaking as one who was a stranger to this story,
    A stranger to what was done. I could not have   220
    Followed the trail far without some clue.
    Now, after the event, I am enrolled as a citizen among citizens,
    And to all of you, people of Cadmus, I say this:
    If any of you knows who is the man
    That killed Laius, son of Labdacus,   225
    I command you to tell me everything.
    If he is afraid, it is best for him to avoid trouble
    By owning up; nothing unpleasant will happen to him
    But he will leave the country, unharmed.
    If anyone knows that the murderer is a stranger   230
    From abroad, then speak out. I will see to it myself
    That you are rewarded, and you will win my gratitude.
    But if you keep silent and, out of fear for a friend
    Or for yourself, you choose to disregard my order,
    Then you must hear what I shall do in consequence: 235
    I forbid any of you in this land, where I hold power
    And sovereign authority, to receive this man into your home –
    Whoever he is – or even to speak to him.
    You may not allow him to join in your prayers to the gods
    Or your sacrifices, nor may you allow him water for purification.   240
    Drive him from your homes, all of you, for
    He is polluting us – as Apollo from his seat in Delphi
    Has now made clear to me.

Oedipus' prayer(s)

In lines 246–51 and 269–75 Oedipus is no longer making a decree, but a prayer to the gods. The distinction is precise: he invokes the gods' support and, in 249–51, places himself under divine authority. Lines 246–51, in square brackets, are considered by some textual critics to be interpolations (later additions by actors or writers).

- Read the speech through with and without the bracketed lines. Which do you find more coherent? (See **One witness, one clue** page 12, and note on 350–1.)

Dramatic irony

Dramatic irony is the effect produced when the audience watching a play, or another character within the play, has a fuller understanding of what is going on than the character involved. The second part of Oedipus' speech is full of such significance for an audience who know his basic story as the man who killed his father and married his mother (see *Background to the story*, pages v–vi). Lines 262 and 264 are perhaps the most striking examples: in 262 we know that Laius' fate was sealed by his *not* remaining childless, and in line 264 Oedipus *is*, of course, fighting for his father – and against himself.

- Find further examples of dramatic irony in the first 268 lines.

Suspense

One of the chief effects of dramatic irony is to create suspense. The conventions of pantomime offer a crude example: when Aladdin is looking for the magic lamp and the audience can all see it behind him, suspense is created until Aladdin finds it. The search for the murderer in *Oedipus Tyrannus* is full of suspense because most of the audience know he is right before their eyes.

260 I sleep and sow my seed where he once sowed his This is the first direct mention (see 70) of Oedipus' marriage to Laius' queen, Jocasta, and the fact that he has children by her.

267–8 Labdacus … Polydorus … Cadmus … Agenor (See *Genealogical table* page viii.) Laius' family tree is well known to Oedipus.

274 may Justice be your ally The personification of abstract nouns (see also 157) is a common feature of Classical literature. Justice (*Dikē*) appears as a goddess in Hesiod's *Theogony*, but in fifth-century Athens some of the audience, familiar with humanistic views of the world centred upon man rather than the traditional Olympian gods, might consider Justice the choice of a sceptic (see **Jocasta's scepticism** page 54).

- What impression of Oedipus' attitude towards religion and the gods have you formed (see also 280–1)?

This is how I will fight – as ally
Of the god and of the man who died.   245
[I also pray that the unknown doer of this deed,
Whether he acted alone or with accomplices,
May wear out his wretched life in abject misery.
What is more, I pray that if in my own home
This man should share my hearth with my full knowledge,   250
I may suffer from the curse that now I've laid on others.]
My charge to you is to observe all this
For me, for the god, and for this land
Which now lies ruined, barren and deserted by the gods.
Even if the god had not taken matters into his own hands,   255
It was wrong for you to leave this crime unpurged so long.
The man who died was your king, a noble man;
You should have conducted a proper search. But now
I hold the authority which he once had,
I sleep and sow my seed where he once sowed his.   260
My children would have shared a mother with his,
If he had not had the misfortune to be childless.
As it is, fate struck him down.
So I shall be fighting for him as if for my own father,
And I shall leave nothing undone in seeking out   265
And finding the author of his murder – the murder
Of the son of Labdacus, who traced his line
Back through Polydorus and Cadmus to Agenor of old.
If any disobey my orders, I pray that the gods
Make their land infertile and their wives barren;   270
That they perish by the same disease
Which now plagues us – or by something worse.
For all you other people of Cadmus, all who find
My words acceptable, may Justice be your ally,
And may all the gods be with you evermore.   275

The Chorus leader

The Chorus leader's response to Oedipus' proclamation helps gauge its effectiveness. His lines, like those of all actors in Greek tragedy, are spoken in verse (*iambics*) rather than sung (*lyrics*, see page 16). (See also First *Stasimon* pages 38–41 for the Chorus' collective response to the prophecy and proclamation.)

- Which of the following words do you think most closely characterise the Chorus leader's response in 276–99: *cooperative, frightened, sullen, respectful, obsequious*? Can you think of others?

278 Apollo started this enquiry As god of both plague and prophecy (see note on 154). The Greek word for enquiry has connotations of an official inquiry. The 'cross-questioning' of Tiresias, who is brought forward as a witness, includes legal language (see notes on 297 and 319–20).

284 Tiresias a native of Thebes, is a confusing figure in mythology. In Homer's *Odyssey* the hero is told to consult the soul of Tiresias, the blind Theban prophet in the underworld (Book *xi*). According to myth he experienced life as both man and woman and was blinded by Hera for his judgement that the female enjoyed sex more than the male. As compensation Zeus granted him the power of prophecy. Tiresias figures in a number of Greek tragedies based in Thebes. In all of these, his understanding is doubted but is never shown to be false.

287 Here too, I have not been slow to act Oedipus again displays *prothūmia* ('readiness to act' 48, and see 69). The sending of people 'twice' (288) suggests particular zeal on Oedipus' part, or sluggishness on that of Tiresias; 'surprised' (289) corresponds to 'worried' (74–5).

- Consider the staging of Tiresias' entry. At what point do you think he should become visible to the audience? Should he move slowly, or try to hurry? (See picture on page 33.)

Further hints?

- Does the exchange of information between the Chorus (who were not there to witness) Creon's report in the Prologue and Oedipus in lines 276–96 add anything to the search?

297 But here is the man to expose him (See **The arrival of Creon** page 10.) The respect of the Thebans for their seer (prophet) is made clear by the Chorus leader's words. Tiresias needs 'bringing' (298) because of his blindness and is accompanied by a boy (444). The Greek word translated as 'expose' is a legal term for cross-questioning and demonstrating the weakness of a case.

CHORUS My lord, held by your curse, I shall speak out.
    I did not kill him, nor can I point to the killer.
    But Apollo started this enquiry; surely it is for him
    To say who committed the crime.

OEDIPUS You are right. But to compel the gods   280
    Against their will – that no man can do.

CHORUS May I suggest what seems to me the next best thing?

OEDIPUS Even if it's third best, don't hold back but tell me.

CHORUS As I understand it, lord Tiresias sees
    Much the same as lord Apollo; anyone looking   285
    Into these matters, my lord, would learn most clearly from him.

OEDIPUS Here too, I have not been slow to act.
    On Creon's advice, I have twice sent people
    To fetch him. I'm surprised he's not here already.

CHORUS Otherwise, we only have old stories that tell us nothing.   290

OEDIPUS What are they? I'll examine any account.

CHORUS He was said to have been killed by travellers.

OEDIPUS I heard that too. But no one can see who did it.

CHORUS If the man has any shred of fear in him,
    Hearing curses like yours, he won't wait long.   295

OEDIPUS If he was not afraid of doing the deed, no words will
      scare him.

CHORUS But here is the man to expose him. These people
    Are now bringing the god's own seer, the only man
    Who carries the living truth inside him.

300–1 everything/That may and may not be known, in heaven and on earth The limits of knowledge constitute a theme essential to the play. A more literal translation of things 'That may and may not be known' is 'things which may be taught and things that are not to be spoken of'. Tiresias transgresses the usual limits of mortal knowledge, the most obvious restriction of which is knowledge of the future, but knowledge of the past and present is also limited – as Oedipus will discover.

302 though you cannot see, you understand Sight is commonly used as a metaphor for knowledge in Greek. Indeed, the Greek root *-id-* (*eid-/oid-*) means both 'see' and 'know'. This gives rise to the paradox of the blind 'having sight' (see, for example, 388–9 and 413). The language of sight and insight is important in this play.

303–4 you are the only/Champion and saviour that we can find Oedipus makes his request to Tiresias in strong terms.
- How would you describe the tone of Oedipus' first words to Tiresias (300–15)? *Polite, flattering, pleading, patronising, sincere, persuasive, familiar*? Try delivering this speech in ways that emphasise some of the above.
- What sort of answer might Oedipus expect?

311 bird-signs, or any other means Taking omens and prophetic readings by watching patterns of bird flight or divination by burnt offerings (see note on 21) was common practice in the fifth century.

316–18 Ah, how terrible it is to be wise… Tiresias' opening words seem paradoxical. They reinforce the idea that the forthcoming encounter will centre around questions of understanding.

319–20 The Greek words for 'come' (*eiselēluthas* 319) and 'Let me go' (*aphes me* 320) are also the technical words for coming into court, and acquittal or release (see notes on 278 and 297).

324 I can see that your words too are not well aimed
- What is Oedipus to make of this? How clear is it to the audience what Tiresias means?

Oedipus' anger
By line 334 Oedipus has lost his temper with Tiresias.
- What provokes this? Is the violence of Oedipus' outburst at line 334 justified?
- Consider ways of making Tiresias as a) provocative and b) calm as possible (using voice, posture, mannerisms). How does this affect your view of Oedipus?

OEDIPUS Tiresias, your mind ranges over everything   300
    That may and may not be known, in heaven and on earth.
    Our city … though you cannot see, you understand
    The sickness that pervades it. My lord, you are the only
    Champion and saviour that we can find.
    In case you haven't heard the news, we sent   305
    To Apollo; his reply was that we will only
    Find deliverance from this sickness if
    We learn for certain who killed Laius, and kill
    The murderers – or send them from this land as exiles.
    Now, don't begrudge us: use your powers of prophecy,   310
    Whether through bird-signs, or any other means.
    Save yourself and your city; save me too;
    Save us from all the pollution caused by this death.
    We are in your hands. The finest work a man can do
    Is to put his abilities at the service of others.   315
TIRESIAS Ah, how terrible it is to be wise
    When wisdom brings no advantage. I knew this well
    But put it from my mind. Otherwise I would not be here.
OEDIPUS What is it? You seem unhappy to have come.
TIRESIAS Let me go home. It will be easier for us both   320
    To bear our burdens, if you do as I say.
OEDIPUS Withholding information? That's neither right
    Nor friendly to this city which has nurtured you.
TIRESIAS I can see that your words too are not well aimed;
    I am trying to avoid the same mistake.   325
OEDIPUS In god's name, do not turn away from us, if you have
      wisdom.
    We are all your suppliants, on our knees before you.
TIRESIAS You all lack understanding. I shall never reveal
    My heavy secret – to say nothing of yours.
OEDIPUS What's that? You know, but will not speak? Do you realise   330
    That you are betraying us and destroying this city?
TIRESIAS I'll be saving us both pain. Why do you persist
    With these useless questions? You won't get an answer from me.
OEDIPUS Damn you, you despicable man! You would move

337 *my* temper Like the English word 'temper', the Greek *orgē* can mean temperament as well as anger (see also 339).

338 your own – your very own Tiresias' words are mysterious and suggestive. Technically, he is referring to Oedipus' temper, but because *orgē* (see above) is feminine, Tiresias sounds in Greek as if he is referring to a woman.

341 Events will take their course, even if I say nothing This is the nature of Tiresias' power – not to alter events, but to foresee them (see also 284–5, 356; for Apollo's power see also note on 1328).

343 I shall say no more
● Why does Tiresias refuse to speak? Is this understandable?

Stichomythia
Characters in Greek drama tend to speak either in speeches or in line-for-line dialogue (*stichomythia*). So far in the play most dialogue has involved characters speaking two lines at a time (*distichomythia*) or more, but the pace intensifies as Oedipus and Tiresias clash.
○ Consider how Sophocles varies the pace throughout the long exchange between Oedipus and Tiresias (300–462).

346 I'll tell you what I think Oedipus launches what at first seems an astonishing accusation against Tiresias. He will return to it at lines 378 and 380–403. Tiresias' response, 'Indeed' (350) is (literally) a devastating one-word question 'True?' (*alēthes?*).

350–1 submit/To your own proclamation Tiresias could be referring to lines 249–51 (see **Oedipus' prayer(s)** page 22), or to 230–2, which have a special reference for Oedipus as a stranger to the city. The accusation that Oedipus is the source of pollution will be repeated in the course of this scene (see **Tiresias' reply** page 32).

354 Are you so shameless as to start that line? Oedipus uses a hunting image: just as a hunter starts an animal from hiding, so Tiresias suddenly, as if from nowhere, looses this attack.

Accusations and abuse
Once the dialogue between Oedipus and Tiresias has become heated, accusations begin to fly (see 347–9, 353 etc.) from both sides. These alternate with exchanges of personal abuse.

356 My strength is in the truth Tiresias is persistent with this line (see also 369, 461). Tiresias, as a blind old man, contrasts starkly with Oedipus, who is young and vigorous.

366–7 a life of shame/With those you love Tiresias has already accused Oedipus of being the murderer of Laius (362). He now seems to make a new, unrelated 'accusation', which strengthens Oedipus' confidence that Tiresias is talking nonsense (368).

A rock to anger. Will you say nothing? 335
Is this how you want to be seen? Stubborn? Intractable?

TIRESIAS You criticise *my* temper. Your eyes are shut
To your own – your very own, yet you find fault with me.

OEDIPUS Who would not lose his temper listening to this?
Your words disgrace this city. 340

TIRESIAS Events will take their course, even if I say nothing.

OEDIPUS Shouldn't you tell me, then, the course they'll take?

TIRESIAS I shall say no more. Do as you will;
Rant and rave as violently as you like.

OEDIPUS Oh, I shall! I understand, and my anger will spare you 345
No details. I'll tell you what I think:
You helped to hatch this business, and took part –
Short of actually killing him. If you weren't blind,
I'd say that this crime was yours alone.

TIRESIAS Indeed? I call upon you to submit 350
To your own proclamation, and from this day
Never again to speak to these people or to me –
As befits the godless polluter of this land.

OEDIPUS Are you so shameless as to start that line?
Do you really think that you can get away with it? 355

TIRESIAS I already have. My strength is in the truth.

OEDIPUS Who taught you this? Not your prophetic skill.

TIRESIAS You did. You forced me to speak against my will.

OEDIPUS What was it you said? Say it again. I want to be sure.

TIRESIAS Didn't you get it the first time? Or are you testing me? 360

OEDIPUS I can't say I really understood. Tell me again.

TIRESIAS I say that you are the murderer you're looking for.

OEDIPUS Vicious slander. You'll regret repeating it.

TIRESIAS Should I say something else, to anger you more?

OEDIPUS As much as you like – but you'll be wasting your words. 365

TIRESIAS I say that, unwittingly, you live a life of shame
With those you love. You cannot see the peril you are in.

OEDIPUS Do you really think you can go on revelling in these
accusations?

Oedipus' accusation against Tiresias

At line 125 Oedipus hinted at a conspiracy, expressing some fear for himself (139–40). Now he accuses Tiresias (347–9) and Creon (378) of plotting against him. In lines 380–403 his accusations take their most coherent form. He accuses Tiresias of being in Creon's pay and both of them of trying to manipulate the situation to displace him.

● Analyse Oedipus' arguments supporting his conspiracy theory in lines 380–403. How coherent are they?

Seeing and seeming

Oedipus sees strength in physical terms, as the ability to see, hear (371) or inflict physical harm (374–5); Tiresias, however (with his contrast of 'now' and 'soon', 372–3), suggests the transience of physical strength and the far greater power of Apollo (377). The difference between seeing and knowing, with their corresponding objects, appearance and truth, is also explored: what appears weak may truly be strong. 'Poor fool' (372) suggests that Tiresias sees Oedipus as just as weak as Oedipus does Tiresias in lines 374–5.

387 swindling sorcerer In Sophocles' *Antigone* Creon levels similar accusations against Tiresias and seers in general. There was a spirit of scepticism about the validity of seers at the time Sophocles produced this play (see **Plague?** page 16, note on 274 and **Jocasta's scepticism** page 54): Aristophanes' comedies *Birds* and *Peace* include quack oracle-mongers who are exposed as frauds. The people of Athens in 413 BC attacked the prophets who had predicted that Sicily would be an easy conquest (Thucydides *viii*, ch. 1) (see also Second *Stasimon* 863–910).

391 How was it…?

● This is a good question. Does Tiresias have an answer to it?

397 ignorant Oedipus Oedipus means to be ironic (to say something other than he means), though in fact these words, recalling 'Famous Oedipus' (8) are some of his most 'truthful'. The striking word-play *mēden* **eidōs Oidi**pous ('*Oedi*pus *know*ing nothing': see note on 302) draws attention to the phrase.

398 I used my wits; I didn't rely on birds A contrast is drawn here between ways of understanding the world: through signs from the gods (see 'bird-signs' 396 and note on 311) and through human understanding (*gnōmē*) (see also 38–9, 43). Oedipus, by his consultation of Delphi and readiness to learn from Tiresias, has shown that he is capable of learning by both means, but here, under provocation and with apparent justification, he celebrates his human powers of reason (see Second *Stasimon* 863–910).

TIRESIAS If there is any strength in the truth, then yes.

OEDIPUS Oh, truth has strength, but not for you. You have
    no strength: 370
  You're blind – ears, mind, eyes – all blind.

TIRESIAS Poor fool, this abuse that now you hurl at me
  Every man here will soon be hurling at you.

OEDIPUS You're wrapped in unending night; you'll never harm
  Me or anyone else who sees the light of day.   375

TIRESIAS No, it's not your fate to fall because of me.
  This is Apollo's concern. He has the power.

OEDIPUS Who invented all this? Was it Creon?

TIRESIAS Creon isn't hurting you – you're hurting yourself.

OEDIPUS Wealth, royal power, and skill surpassing skill –   380
  In life with all its heavy load of envy,
  What resentment you have stored up in you, if
  For the sake of this power, which the city placed
  In my hands as a gift – I did not ask for it –
  For this, Creon – who was from the first my trusted friend –   385
  Steals up on me and wants to overthrow me.
  He's got this swindling sorcerer in his pay,
  A money-grubbing trickster, with a good eye
  For gain, but blind when it comes to prophecy.
  Come on, tell me, when have you proved clear-sighted?   390
  How was it that when the singing bitch was here
  You said nothing to these citizens to set them free?
  And yet her riddle was not for any passer-by
  To solve; it required a seer.
  Yet you were not conspicuous for your understanding,   395
  From bird-signs or from the gods. Then *I* came along,
  I, ignorant Oedipus, and I stopped her.
  I used my wits; I didn't rely on birds.
  And it's me you're trying to throw out, thinking that you
  Will stand at Creon's side when the throne is his.   400

403 You'd learn the hard way Oedipus seems to be restraining himself from physical violence against the seer (see note on 1153), perhaps motivating the intervention from the Chorus.

The Chorus leader intervenes

The Chorus leader in Greek tragedies frequently comments blandly in the course of an *agōn* or debate (see **Agōn?** page 34). In this case, he seems to show excellent judgement (see also 631–3).

Tiresias' reply

Tiresias begins with a declaration of his right to speech, by no means always a 'given' in the court of an autocrat, but he also uses the metaphor of slavery in respect of Oedipus' rule, claiming servitude only to the god Apollo.

● Is this an attack, or does it reflect well, on Oedipus' style of kingship (see also 574–81)?

Before repeating his attack on Oedipus (see note on 366–7), Tiresias briefly dismisses Oedipus' accusation of conspiracy with Creon in line 411 (contrast with the length of Creon's counter-argument in lines 583–615).

412 You mocked me for my blindness (see 371, 374)

415 Without realising it Tiresias emphasises Oedipus' ignorance (366 'unwittingly', 413 'you cannot see').

417 The curse of your mother and father The 'curse' here is something like an avenging spirit (see note on 472). The Greek includes the word *deinopous,* literally 'terrible of foot', recalling Oedipus' name, *Oidipous*; it is one of many examples of word-play (see **'Swollen-foot'** page 76). In some versions of the Oedipus story, Oedipus is presented as the victim of, in particular, his father's folly or wickedness; in this play he suffers as a result of his parents' fear and/or cruelty (see 718–19), but there is no other explicit mention of a curse.

I think you and the man behind all this will regret
Your attempted purge. If you didn't look so senile,
You'd learn the hard way what your 'wisdom' amounts to.
CHORUS It seems to us that his words were spoken in anger,
But so were yours, Oedipus. 405
This is not what we need. What we must consider
Is how best to unravel the god's oracular words.
TIRESIAS You may be king, but I have equal right
To match you word for word. I have *this* power.
I am not your slave, but Apollo's, 410
And I won't be cast as Creon's protégé.
You mocked me for my blindness, but I tell you this:
You may have eyes, but you cannot see your danger –
Where you're living, who you're living with.
Do you know whose son you are? Without realising it, 415
You're the bane of your family, both dead and here on earth.
The curse of your mother and father, a double blow,
Will one day drive you stumbling from this land.
Now you see clearly, but then you will see darkness.

John Gielgud as Tiresias in the BBC production of Oedipus the King, *1985.*

Prophetic words

Prophetic words were often obscure or riddling (see **The Delphic oracle** page 8), though, like most riddles, the meaning is often transparent once it is understood. Tiresias' words, which may not be wholly clear even to the audience, are impenetrable to Oedipus, who dismisses Tiresias as 'a fool' (433).

● What gives Tiresias' words in lines 413–25 such a sense of power and mystery?

420, 422 harbour … mooring These nautical images give the sense of someone adrift, exposed to danger. Sailors can judge what constitutes a 'sound mooring' only by experience and by trusting their senses (see note on 104).

421 Cithaeron A mountain in the range separating Thebes from Athens (see map, page vii). It comes to loom large in this play.

426 Now fling mud at Creon The Greek idiom is the same as the English.

430 To hell with you! The Greek is literally 'to destruction'.

437 Who? Wait; who are my parents? This is the first moment we see Oedipus express any kind of doubt. Lines 779–88 may help us to see why.

438 This day Most surviving Greek tragedies have 'unity of place' (the action is set in one place) and 'unity of time' (events take place in a day). *Oedipus Tyrannus* is a classic example, breath-taking in its swiftness of action (see also 351, 615 and **Reversal of fortune** page 80).

440 Aren't you a champion at solving those? Tiresias' quick retort seems malicious – but irresistible. Oedipus' fame (8) was the result of his victory in solving the riddle of the Sphinx (see page 6 and 391).

● How far does Tiresias control his feelings in this scene? Is he simply the 'slave' of Apollo (410) or does he respond personally?

442 luck The Greek, *Tychē*, is often personified as a goddess, Fortune/ Chance/Luck (see notes on 274 and 977). Later Oedipus will use the same word when he describes himself as 'the child of Fortune' (1080). So far Oedipus' career has been characterised by great good fortune but *Tychē*, like 'luck', can be good or bad.

Agōn?

In an *agōn* or debate characters put forward and defend different sides of an argument (see also 543–82). The balanced pair of speeches at 380–403 and 408–28 are typical, but there is something 'dysfunctional' about this *agōn*: the lack of understanding of Tiresias' words by Oedipus makes coherent debate virtually impossible.

Is there any place that will not harbour your cries?   420
Soon all Cithaeron will resound with them,
When you understand the truth of your wedding – no sound
    mooring
For your house, though you sailed into it after a fair voyage.
You have no idea of the host of other horrors
That will put you on a level with your children.   425
Now fling mud at Creon, and at my words.
There's no man living who will ever be
As miserably crushed as you will be.

OEDIPUS Must I endure this, coming from him? Must I listen?
To hell with you! Quickly, go back again   430
Away from this house, and get back where you came from.

TIRESIAS I wouldn't have come if you hadn't invited me.

OEDIPUS If I'd known you were going to talk like a fool, I wouldn't
Have been in a hurry to summon you to my house.

TIRESIAS You may think me a fool, but the parents   435
Who gave you birth thought me wise enough.

OEDIPUS Who? Wait; who are my parents?

TIRESIAS This day will prove your birth and your destruction.

OEDIPUS Nothing you say is clear; you talk in riddles.

TIRESIAS Aren't you a champion at solving those?   440

OEDIPUS Mock if you like, but that's the source of my power.

TIRESIAS Yes, this was your luck, and now it has destroyed you.

OEDIPUS But if I saved this city, I don't care.

TIRESIAS Then I'll leave. Boy, take me home.

OEDIPUS Yes, take him. Here, you just obstruct our path.   445
Once you're gone, you'll give us no more trouble.

447 I'll go when I've said what I came here for The scene seemed about to close at 446, but Tiresias speaks one last time, again in riddling language. This time he uses the third person, but in many ways his meaning is far clearer and more frightening.

Oedipus' response
Oedipus makes no reply and gives no sign of having understood anything Tiresias has said beyond, perhaps, line 362 (see 747). This was enough, it seems, for him to judge the nature of Tiresias' attacks and to discount them. Oedipus' failure to 'hear' Tiresias has seemed theatrically implausible to some; it is possible that Oedipus enters the palace while Tiresias is speaking or that Tiresias begins to leave during the speech, though 'Go inside' (460) seems inconsistent with this view (see **Stage directions** page 20).

○ What is the most dramatically effective moment for Oedipus to make his exit?

Review of the First Episode
By the end of the First Episode the audience have been told unequivocally that Oedipus is the murderer of Laius, his father, and that he is the husband of his mother and therefore brother of his own children. Oedipus' self-blinding and exile have also been foretold. Sophocles strains the powers of dramatic irony almost to the limit by asking the audience to accept that what they have heard so clearly, Oedipus has not heard at all. The effect of all this is greatly to increase the tension as Oedipus' fall seems so close. From this point on, we wait to see how Oedipus will learn the truth.

● When you have read the whole play, consider what would be lost if this scene were omitted.

○ In 483 the Chorus describe their response to the seer's words as 'confused and frightened'; consider ways of making this scene as 'frightening' as possible. Would sound or lighting effects contribute to or undermine the scariness of the scene in a modern production?

TIRESIAS I'll go when I've said what I came here for.
I'm not afraid of you; you can't destroy me.
Here's what I say to you. This man you seek
With all your threats and proclamations   450
For the murder of Laius, he is here –
A stranger who's settled here, or so it's said.
Soon he'll be revealed as a native Theban,
But his change of fortune will bring him little joy.
Now he is rich and can see, but he'll be a blind beggar,   455
Feeling his way with a stick to a foreign land.
Father and brother at once to his own children
He'll be revealed; and also son and husband
To the woman who bore him; sowing the same furrow
As his father, and his father's murderer. Go inside   460
And work this out; and if you find I've lied,
Say then that prophecy has given me no wisdom.

Tiresias is led on stage.
Greg Hicks in The
Oedipus Plays, National
Theatre, London, 1996.

FIRST CHORAL ODE (1ST *STASIMON*) (463–512)

All choral odes after the entry ode (*parodos*) are performed in the *orchēstra*. They are known as *stasima* or 'standing choruses'.

The Chorus wonder about the identity of the killer of Laius and consider his fate (463–82). They reflect on Tiresias' allegations against Oedipus and express loyalty to their king (483–512).

463 Who is the man…? The Chorus respond with awe to Oedipus' proclamation (216–75) about the oracle's words (see note on 151).

469–70 son of Zeus, /Armed with fire and lightning Apollo, armed with weapons usually associated with his father (see note on 151).

472 the avenging goddesses The Erinyes or Eumenides ('Kindly Ones' – an 'apotropaic' name intended to avert evil). They pursue their victims relentlessly to exact retribution for crimes committed.

475 from snowy Parnassus, shines out See **The Delphic oracle** page 8 and **Clear instructions?** page 10.

477 Like a bull Man was seen as being uniquely different from animals in requiring a *polis* (city/state) (see **The consequences** page 20). The wild landscape recalling Tiresias' words at 420–1 emphasises the isolation of the killer.

479 Forlorn The Chorus' remarkable sympathy for the cause of all their suffering foreshadows a shift in emphasis in the play as hunter becomes hunted. Lines 480–2 contribute to this effect, building on ideas already present in Tiresias' words (see 420–8, 456).

481 earth's navel See **The Delphic oracle** page 8.

485 I neither accept his words nor reject them (see also 500) Choruses in Greek tragedies are often cautious about committing themselves to one side of an argument (see 404–7). Moreover, Tiresias the seer is a man, not a god; like the priest in the Prologue the Chorus are unsure in dealing with a man who seemed to be favoured with understanding from the gods. See also lines 708–9.

487 I flutter with hope The identification of the Chorus with their king is striking, particularly in view of his history as an 'outsider'.

492 the family of Labdacus and the son of Polybus There is irony here. Polybus was known as Oedipus' father (see 774, 941 etc.).

493 A touchstone is used for testing the purity of metal; pure gold marks the stone with a yellow streak, giving *reliable* evidence of its purity. The same image is used at lines 509–10.

CHORUS   Who is the man denounced
By the oracular rock of Delphi –
The man who with bloody hands   465
Accomplished the unspeakable?
Time for him to set foot in flight,
Outracing storm-swift horses,
For the son of Zeus,
Armed with fire and lightning,   470
Leaps upon him,
And the avenging goddesses,
Dreadful and unerring, are on his trail.

A new revelation,
The word from snowy Parnassus, shines out: 475
Everyone must track down the unknown man.
Like a bull he roams
The wild woods, the mountain caves, the rocks,
Forlorn, with forlorn tread, an outcast,
Trying to keep away from the oracles   480
That come from earth's navel, but ever-living
They hover over him.

I was frightened, confused and frightened
By the wise seer.
I neither accept his words nor reject them;   485
I don't know what to say.
I flutter with hope
But I cannot see
What's here or what's to come.
I know of no established quarrel,   490
Either before or now,
Between the family of Labdacus and the son of Polybus,
A touchstone for me to test
The public reputation of Oedipus,
Though I want to help the family of Labdacus   495
In the matter of this mysterious death.

507 The winged girl See **The riddle of the Sphinx** page 6.

509–10 he passed the test… (see note on line 493) 'He was seen to be wise' seems phrased to emphasise the way humans judge the world.

Review of the First *Stasimon*

- Just as some of the language of the First Episode was reminiscent of an Athenian court (see 278, 297, 319–20 etc.), so the Chorus seem to play the part of a jury in this ode (see especially 490–512). Who is 'on trial'? What arguments do the Chorus consider before reasserting their loyalty to Oedipus?
○ Trace the different moods in this ode; how might these qualities be brought out in performance?

SECOND EPISODE (513–862)

Creon's return

As the Chorus' song ends, Creon rushes into the *orchēstra* to answer the 'charges'. As in the First Episode, technical language of the Athenian courts is frequent in the *agōn* (see page 34) that ensues.

514 king Oedipus Creon uses the word *tyrannos* for 'king'. Oedipus has been given supreme power after the murder of the hereditary king Laius, who apparently died without an heir. Sole rulers who came to power illegally were called *tyrannoi* – 'tyrants' (although Oedipus uses the word *tyrannis* of Laius' reign in 129). The Greek word indicated status rather than behaviour and could have good associations, even for an audience who prided themselves on their democratic government. The use of *Tyrannus* in the title of this play to differentiate it from *Oedipus at Colonus* postdates Sophocles.

519 It's not a simple matter Creon is concerned to defend his reputation. The word repeated as 'traitor' is simply *kakos*, which has a wide range of meanings (e.g. bad/base/evil/worthless/cowardly).
- Was Oedipus justified in attacking Creon? How easy would it be for him to back down, given the public (525) nature of his words?
- From what you have learned of Oedipus so far in this play, what response might you expect from him now?

530 I do not know. What our rulers do is not for me to see The Chorus acknowledge limits to their understanding, separating themselves from those with the burden of power. The *skēnē* representing the royal palace creates a physical divide in this play between the public affairs of the city and the private affairs of the palace.

Zeus and Apollo are wise;
They know the ways of mortals.
But as for men,
There is no true way of judging   500
Whether a seer wins the prize over me.
One man may surpass another
In wisdom;
But I shall never say that the critics are right
Until I see their words proved true.   505
We all witnessed how
The winged girl
Attacked him that time
And he passed the test.
He was seen to be wise and brought joy to this city.   510
So I shall never think him
Guilty of any evil.

CREON Men of the city, I hear that terrible words
    Are spoken against me by king Oedipus.
    That's why I'm here. I can't bear it. If in this crisis   515
    Which now we face he thinks that I have done
    Anything to harm him, by either word or deed,
    Then I have no desire to prolong my life
    Bearing such a reputation. It's not a simple matter,
    The injury done to me by what he's said: 520
    There's nothing worse than hearing the city call me traitor,
    And hearing 'traitor' from you and from my friends.
CHORUS This was his accusation, but perhaps
    Anger, rather than considered judgement, forced it out.
CREON And was it publicly stated that my advice   525
    Had persuaded the seer to speak his lying words?
CHORUS This was said, but I do not know with what intention.
CREON Was his look steady, and was his mind steady
    When this accusation was spoken out against me?
CHORUS I do not know. What our rulers do is not for me to see. 530
    [But here he comes himself out of the palace.]

535 it's obvious! The 'clarity' of Oedipus' views on the 'conspiracy' is impressive. As his opening lines indicate, time for reflection has intensified rather than softened his angry belief in Creon's treachery.
- Does Oedipus introduce any new grounds for suspicion?
- Do you find his behaviour towards Creon psychologically convincing? How far does Oedipus seem in control?

541 Hunting for absolute power We have seen a hunting metaphor used before of the search for the murderer (109–11, 221, 476); the trails seem to cross as Oedipus accuses Creon of his own independent hunt for kingship.

545 a clever speaker Oedipus, who is referring to Creon, uses words to fight Creon much as Tiresias used them against him; Creon is hardly allowed to speak. A sarcastic tone is created here by the way that Oedipus mimics Creon's words (547–52).

553–4 what/Do you say I've done to hurt you? Oedipus answers Creon's questions with a series of questions of his own (555–68) (see also note on 112).
- What tone should Oedipus' questioning take? How might the respective positions, stances, movements and voices of the actors contribute to the drama of this interrogation?

OEDIPUS You there! What brought you here? Are you really so brash
As to show your face by coming to my house,
When I am the man you clearly want to kill
And rob – it's obvious! – of my royal power.   535
Now tell me, in the name of the gods, was it cowardice or folly
That you saw in me when you planned these acts against me?
Did you think I wouldn't notice your stealthy deed
Creeping up on me – or that I'd find out, and not defend myself?
Isn't this attempt of yours a foolish one –   540
Hunting for absolute power without wealth or friends,
When men and money are needed to catch that prey?

CREON Do this for me – you know you should: in response to your words
Give me an equal hearing, then make an informed judgement.

OEDIPUS You are a clever speaker, but I am poor at learning –   545
From you; I've found you to be my enemy – and a burden to me.

CREON Listen first to what I have to say…

OEDIPUS To say you're not a traitor – I've no wish to hear.

CREON If you believe that stubbornness is worth having
Without good sense, then you are wrong.   550

OEDIPUS And if *you* believe that you can harm a kinsman
And not face the penalty, then *you* are wrong.

CREON I agree with you; what you say is right. But what
Do you say I've done to hurt you? Tell me this.

OEDIPUS Did you or did you not seek to persuade me   555
To send someone to fetch that pious seer?

CREON I wouldn't advise you differently even now.

OEDIPUS How long a period has elapsed now since Laius…

CREON Did what? I do not understand your question.

OEDIPUS Disappeared, the victim of a murderous attack?   560

CREON Long years – an age, if one were to measure it.

OEDIPUS At that time, was this seer engaged in his craft?

CREON He was just as wise, and was equally held in honour.

OEDIPUS Did he at that time mention me at all?

CREON No – at least, never in my company.   565

OEDIPUS Did you people not hold an inquiry about the dead man?

CREON We did; of course we did. But we heard nothing.

OEDIPUS And why did this 'clever' man not speak out at the time?

569 I do not know (see also 571) Creon's words are identical to those of the Chorus at 530. Both, in refusing to comment on what they do not know, draw attention to the fact that this is precisely what Oedipus is doing now.

● Does Creon's response appear provocative?

574 Only you know if this is his story A tactful and cautious response. Creon seems to be careful not to say, 'Only you know whether his story is true.'

574–5 I've the right/To learn from you (see also 408–9) In talking of Tiresias' 'human knowledge' Oedipus spoke of things 'that may and may not be known' (see note on 300–1). The language of teaching and learning plays an important part in this episode (see 545) and the process by which Oedipus has cross-examined Creon is a form of learning. In Plato's dialogues Socrates is shown using a similar technique.

○ As the roles of 'teacher' and 'pupil' are reversed (lines 577–81), consider how you might stage these lines to highlight similarities and differences between the situation here and at lines 555–68. Who appears to win this 'round'?

576 proved a murderer
● Where do the audience's sympathies lie at this moment?

Creon's 'apologia' (speech of defence)
Creon's speech is measured and careful: he sets out his thesis, that absolute power has no attractions for him, and then defends it. His tone may at first seem dry and excessively cautious (see note on 574), but it builds up to an emotional appeal.

● Which do you consider the strongest and weakest arguments in Creon's speech of defence (583–615)?

CREON I do not know; and when I don't understand I prefer to keep
      quiet.
OEDIPUS This much you do know – and would be wise to say –   570
CREON What? If I know, I'll not refuse to speak.
OEDIPUS That, had he not gone along with you, he'd never
      Have spoken of *my* having murdered Laius.
CREON Only you know if this is his story; but I've the right
      To learn from you, as you have learnt from me.   575
OEDIPUS Learn all you want; I'll not be proved a murderer.
CREON Well, then – you married my sister and have her as your wife?
OEDIPUS There's no denying what you're asking me.
CREON And you rule this land together, equally?
OEDIPUS Anything she wants, she gets from me.   580
CREON And am I not third equal to the two of you?
OEDIPUS In that, you are shown to be a treacherous friend.
CREON No, not if you reason it out for yourself as I have.
      Consider this first: do you think that anyone
      Would choose to rule and be afraid, rather than   585
      Sleep untroubled, while having no less power?
      I at any rate have never myself desired
      To be a king rather than do what a king does;
      Nor does anyone else who knows good sense.
      As it is, I have all I want from you with no anxiety,   590
      But if *I* were ruler, I'd be doing many things I didn't want to.
      How then could kingship be more pleasant for me
      Than a position of command and power without the pain?
      I am not so utterly deluded
      As to want honours that do not also bring profit.   595
      Now, all wish me joy; now everyone greets me;
      Now, those who want something from you call on me:
      For that way lies their best hope of success.
      Why should I take on your power, and relinquish mine?
      [No mind that's sound could contemplate betrayal.]   600
      I am no lover of this kind of scheming,
      And I could not bear to support another's treachery.

614–15 time alone … a single day (see note on 438)

● Consider what Creon means by this.

617 Those who are quick in their thinking are liable to stumble The Chorus are praising Creon's speech, but their 'gnomic comment' (a comment expressing general wisdom) brings to mind Oedipus with his readiness to act and quick wit (see 69–70, 287–9, 346–9, 378).

623 dead, not just an exile The clemency in Oedipus' proclamation (see 228–9) is nowhere to be found in his words to his brother-in-law.

● Do you think this harsh treatment is excessive? Does Oedipus seem to be more motivated by anger or by a sense of betrayal? Can you explain his response?

Antilabē (see *Stichomythia* page 28)

As the urgency of the argument intensifies, so does the pace. This effect is created by the way the two men pick up on each other's words, but also by the brevity of their utterances. This staccato exchange of half-lines (626–9) is called *antilabē*. There is another sudden change of pace with the entry of Jocasta (see also 1173–6 and 1516–22).

To test my words, first you may go to Delphi
And learn if I gave you a true report of the oracle;
Then, if you find that I and the soothsayer   605
Have plotted something together, do not convict
And kill me just by your own vote, but by mine as well;
But do not charge me on an unproven suspicion, without evidence.
It cannot be right to think either that bad
People are good or that good are bad, without reason.   610
[To cast out a good friend, I say, is just the same
As throwing away one's own life, one's dearest possession.]
In time you'll come to know this truth for sure
Since time alone reveals the man who is just.
The criminal can be discovered in a single day.   615
CHORUS Good words, my lord, for one taking care not to fall.
    Those who are quick in their thinking are liable to stumble.
OEDIPUS When the man who secretly plots against me is quick
    To move, then I too must respond with quick thinking.
    If I do nothing but wait for him, he will have achieved   620
    His aim, while I will have missed my opportunity.
CREON So what do you want? To throw me out of this land?
OEDIPUS Not at all. I want you dead, not just an exile.
CREON By that you show what it is to feel resentment.
OEDIPUS You speak as one who'll neither yield nor trust me.   625
CREON Yes, for I see you have no sense.
OEDIPUS   For myself I have.
CREON But you should for me as well.
OEDIPUS   But you're a traitor.
CREON What if you understand nothing?
OEDIPUS   Still I must rule.
CREON Not if you're ruling badly.
OEDIPUS   O city, my city!
CREON The city is mine as well, not yours alone.   630
CHORUS Stop this, my lords; just when you need her I see
    Jocasta coming here out of the house; with her help
    You should settle this quarrel that's broken out between you.

The entry of Jocasta

Jocasta, Oedipus' wife and, as the audience must all now be aware, mother (see *Background to the Story*, page v) suddenly appears from the palace.

● As the audience is faced for the first time with these two characters together on stage, is any hint given as to the dual nature of their relationship? How 'maternal' are Jocasta's opening lines (634–48)?

○ In modern theatre and, especially, on screen there is often great emphasis on realism. Consider Jocasta's appearance in this light: she must be significantly older than Oedipus, to whom she has been married for long enough to produce four children (see note on 1460).

○ The ancient Greek theatre used masks which could communicate only one or two characteristics. Which do you think are most important for Jocasta?

Oaths

In lines 647 and 653 references are made to an oath sworn by Creon in 644–5 which emphasise its significance. Creon does not invoke any gods specifically to witness his oath, but his sister speaks of the sanctity of his words. Perjury (swearing a false oath or breaking an oath) was generally viewed very seriously in fifth-century Athens.

○ Consider ways of highlighting this oath in performance.

FIRST *KOMMOS* (649–96)

The actors and Chorus no longer speak in iambics (see **The Chorus leader** page 24) but sing to musical accompaniment in *lyric* metre. This is called a *kommos*. Such a change in metre generally creates a more intense or emotionally charged atmosphere (see also Second *Kommos* 1297–1366). It is not clear whether the full Chorus sing, or the Chorus leader alone. The arrangement is symmetrical, like that of the major choral odes (see *Parodos*, page 16), but *strophē* is separated from *antistrophē* by nine lines of iambics (669–77).

In the strophē *(649–68) the Chorus, in dialogue with Oedipus, urge him to spare Creon; Oedipus grudgingly gives way and Creon, still aggrieved, leaves (669–77); in the* antistrophē *(678–96) the Chorus are in dialogue with Jocasta until lines 690–6 when they speak to Oedipus, reaffirming their gratitude and loyalty to him (compare First* Stasimon*).*

JOCASTA What folly is this? You sorry pair, have you both lost
Control of your tongues? Are you not ashamed   635
When our land is sick to be stirring up private troubles?
Into the house – and you, Creon, back to your home.
Don't create a major grievance out of nothing.

CREON Sister, your husband thinks he has the right
To treat me terribly, condemning me to one of two fates –   640
Either to throw me out of my land, or take and kill me.

OEDIPUS Agreed. I caught him planning harm, my lady,
Against my person, using evil arts.

CREON May I forfeit all happiness, and die accursed,
If I have wronged you in any way, as you accuse me.   645

JOCASTA In the name of the gods, believe his words, Oedipus,
First, respect this oath he has sworn to the gods,
Then me, and all these people here with you.

CHORUS   Think, and be ready to do as she says,
                        My lord, I beg –   650

OEDIPUS   What do you want me to concede?

CHORUS   He was no foolish child before;
                  Now his oath gives him stature – respect him.

OEDIPUS   You know what you want?

CHORUS   I know.

OEDIPUS   Then tell me: what do you mean?   655

CHORUS   When a friend is on oath, do not dishonour him
            By throwing at him a charge whose words are unproven.

659 death, or exile If Oedipus is right about Creon's disloyalty, he is not overstating the consequences.

- Do you think that Oedipus is convinced by the Chorus and Jocasta that his suspicions were unfounded or, by backing down, is he subjecting himself to further danger? Why does he not follow up Creon's suggestions at 603–15?
- Do you think that 'Your words' (671) refers to the Chorus leader or to Jocasta?

674–5 A nature like yours/Is rightly hardest for itself to bear
Creon does not go quietly. Like Tiresias in 408–28 he speaks back to Oedipus and is critical of his temper (see also 334–46, 698 and **Oedipus' anger** page 26).

677 Not understood by you, but secure in these men's understanding Once again Oedipus stands apart from others because of what he does and doesn't understand. The divided line 676 gives a good impression of the strained relationship between the two men.

The character of Creon

- In Anouilh's *Antigone*, a version of Sophocles' play of the same name, aspects of Creon's character seem to have been influenced by Sophocles' *Oedipus Tyrannus* as much as by his *Antigone*. Compare the following character sketch with the impressions of Creon's character you have so far formed: 'That grey-haired, powerfully built man sitting lost in thought … is Creon, the King. His face is lined. He is tired. He practises the difficult art of a leader of men. When he was younger, when Oedipus was King … he was different. He loved music, bought rare manuscripts, was a kind of art patron. He would while away whole afternoons in the antique shops of this city of Thebes.'

679 inside the house The same question of public and private speech is raised here as in 91–2. See also 525 and note on 530. The action naturally remains in front of the *skēnē* (stage-building) as the Chorus give Jocasta what information they feel they can.

690 this is not the first time that I've said it The Chorus have asserted their loyalty earlier in the play (see 485–512), though not directly to Oedipus. There, as here, they base their trust on their experience.

OEDIPUS Make no mistake; in seeking this, for me
You're seeking death, or exile from this land.

CHORUS   No, by the god who is above all gods,   660
The sun, may I perish utterly, deserted
By gods and friends, if that is my intention.
The death of my land is fate enough for me;   665
My heart will wear out, if to existing troubles
Are added new ones from the two of you.

OEDIPUS Well, let him go – even if this ensures my death
Or the disgrace of forced ejection from this land.   670
Your words, not his, stir my compassion by their pity;
He, wherever he is, will incur my hate.

CREON *You* hate to give in, that's clear, and weigh others down
With your anger, going beyond all limits. A nature like yours
Is rightly hardest for itself to bear.   675

OEDIPUS Leave me alone. Get out of here.

CREON   I'll go;
Not understood by you, but secure in these men's understanding.

CHORUS   Lady, why do you hesitate
To take him inside the house?

JOCASTA   I want to find out what happened.   680

CHORUS   Words led to ignorant conjecture.
Wounding injustice followed.

JOCASTA From both of them?

CHORUS   Yes.

JOCASTA   And what was said?

CHORUS To me it seems enough – more than enough,   685
As I think of our land – to let this matter rest.

OEDIPUS You see where this leads you? Good man though you are
In your intentions, you weaken and blunt my feelings.

CHORUS   My lord, this is not the first time that I've said it: 690
You must know that I would appear out of my mind,
Without a scrap of wisdom, if I rejected you.

695–6 a fair wind … pilot A nautical image again of Oedipus keeping his ship on a straight course (see notes on 39 and 104).

● What do the Chorus mean when they say that Oedipus has 'brought a fair wind'?

697 my lord Jocasta uses the same form as the Chorus do (650, 690 etc.), referring to him as 'ruler' (*anax*); correspondingly, both Oedipus and the Chorus refer to Jocasta as 'lady' – the Greek word (*gunē*) simply means 'woman' or 'wife' (642, 678 etc.).

700 these men The Chorus have played an important part in this episode, apparently showing wise judgement and loyalty to their ruler while at the same time managing to preserve their integrity (530, 685–6) and helping to influence Oedipus (656–7 etc.).

● Does Oedipus' sneer at 700 seem deserved?

704 Has he personal knowledge? Jocasta's interest in the grounds for Creon's accusation, rather than any outright refutation of it, gives Oedipus the chance to express his theory about Tiresias and leads to an expression of her own belief, that no mortal has any special knowledge of things that 'may not be known' (301).

Jocasta's story
Jocasta's words are intended to put Oedipus' mind at ease, by assuring him of the unreliability of oracles. As evidence, she refers to the second oracle of the play concerning Laius and herself (713–14). In an earlier version of the Oedipus story by Aeschylus (see *Background to the story*, page v) this oracle was a warning to Laius not to father a child lest it kill him; but in a frenzy of passion, Laius disregarded the warning and so sired his own murderer. In Sophocles' version the suggestion that Laius might avoid fathering the child is not explicit.

Infant exposure
Ancient myths and legends are full of stories of babies who escape death and rise to greatness in later life: such 'reversals of fortune' (see page 80) make good stories, like those of Paris, Moses, Cyrus the Great and Romulus and Remus; Euripides' tragedy *Ion* offers another example (see note on 1059). Infant exposure was not, however, simply the stuff of stories in the ancient world: a child who was deformed, weak, illegitimate or of the wrong gender might legitimately be 'exposed'. We cannot tell how widely practised this was in fifth-century Athens, but infanticide of this kind was not as abhorrent as it is in the modern western world. The pinning of Oedipus' ankles (718, 1034–5 and **'Swollen-foot'** page 76) may be a detail specific to Sophocles' version of the story.

When my dear land was in trouble before and adrift,
You brought a fair wind and set her on a straight course: 695
Be as good a pilot to us again now.

JOCASTA In the name of the gods, will *you* explain to me, my lord,
What was it that made you so very angry?

OEDIPUS I'll tell you. I've more respect for you, wife, than for
these men. 700
It was Creon – and the plot he had formed against me.

JOCASTA Tell me – a clear account of the quarrel and your charge
against him.

OEDIPUS He says that I am the murderer of Laius.

JOCASTA Has he personal knowledge? Or has he learnt this from
someone else?

OEDIPUS He sent the seer to do his evil work; 705
As for him, his words are entirely his own.

JOCASTA Free yourself now from these things you talk of.
Listen to me, and learn from me that no one
Who is mortal has the power of prophecy.
I'll quickly show you evidence of this. 710
An oracle once came to Laius – I won't say
From Apollo himself, but from his underlings –
Saying that it would be his fate to be killed
By any child born to the two of us;
But he was killed, or so the story went, by strangers, 715
By robbers, at a place where three roads meet.
As for the child, he was not three days old
When Laius bound his ankles tight together
And had others throw him out on the trackless mountain.
Apollo then accomplished neither end: 720
The child was not his father's murderer, nor did Laius
Suffer the terror he feared at the hands of his son.

Jocasta's scepticism

Someone who doubts the truth about religion may be called sceptical (see note on 274). Jocasta claims that the prophecy to Laius has been proved wrong ('Apollo then accomplished neither end', 720), but she seems careful at lines 709 and 712 to distinguish between the god and interpreters of his words (see also notes on 897–902 and 910).

- Are Jocasta's religious views in lines 707–25 consistent? Would you describe her as a sceptic?

730 a place where three roads meet (also 716 and 733–4) The place, once described by the great Victorian commentator Jebb as 'a scene of inexpressible grandeur and desolation', is still identifiable.

738 O Zeus, what are you planning to do to me? For a second time (see 437) Oedipus is thrown; placing himself in the context of Zeus' divine order, he suddenly sees his own vulnerability.

740 Don't ask me yet Oedipus seeks privacy and time to learn the truth. The audience learn these new details of Laius' death for the first time and, like Jocasta, wait to see Oedipus' reaction. Interestingly, Jocasta does not mention the one detail provided by the witness that was revealed earlier in the play (122–3; see 851).

- Why do you think these details did not emerge earlier (see also 758–62)?

754 Ah, it is all too clear now! Oedipus' one question (750–1) appears to confirm his suspicions. Nevertheless, he continues to search for information and, at last (765), asks for the witness to be brought (see **One witness, one clue** page 12).

Yet that is what the words of seers marked out.
So pay them no attention; whatever the god
Needs to track down, he'll easily reveal himself. 725
OEDIPUS Listening to you just then, lady, I felt
My mind roam back, a stirring of my thoughts.
JOCASTA What is troubling you? Why these anxious words?
OEDIPUS I thought that this was what I heard you say – that Laius
Was cut down at a place where three roads meet. 730
JOCASTA Yes, that was what was said – and is the story still.
OEDIPUS And where is this place? Where did all this happen?
JOCASTA Phocis, the land is called; one road from Delphi,
Another from Daulia – they lead to the same place.
OEDIPUS How long a time has passed since these events? 735
JOCASTA Shortly before you emerged as ruler of
This land, the news was reported to the city.
OEDIPUS O Zeus, what are you planning to do to me?
JOCASTA What is it, Oedipus? What is troubling you?
OEDIPUS Don't ask me yet. What did Laius look like? 740
How was he built? Tell me how old he was.
JOCASTA He was dark, with hair beginning to go grey.
In build, not much different from you.
OEDIPUS Oh, what a wretch I am! It seems I have just
Exposed myself to a terrible curse, without knowing it. 745
JOCASTA What do you mean? It frightens me to look at you.
OEDIPUS I've a terrible feeling that the seer can see.
Just tell me one thing more, and you'll make it clearer.
JOCASTA I am frightened, but I will tell you what I know.
OEDIPUS Was he travelling light, or did he have a large 750
Escort of armed men, as a king might have?
JOCASTA There were five men in all; one of them was
A herald; just one carriage, with Laius in it.
OEDIPUS Ah, it is all too clear now! But who was he,
The man who brought this news to you, my lady? 755

764 and indeed much more Jocasta is unspecific as to why the slave's services were so valued, but see 1038–53.

767 My lady See note on 697.

Oedipus' story

Oedipus begins his story naturally, by going back to the beginning. He gives his parents' names and hints modestly at their status in Corinth (776, see 939–41) before referring to the chance event (779–80) that was to change his life. Two further mentions of his mother and father (783–4, 787) contribute to a brief impression of life before Oedipus' journey to Delphi (see also 1023). We have already seen how history is gradually revealed in the course of this play (see notes on 8, 35; lines 260–1); in 774–813 the story goes back to Oedipus' earliest memories and continues until just before he meets the Sphinx and establishes himself in Thebes.

Franco Citti as Oedipus and Silvana Mangano as Jocasta in Pier Paolo Pasolini's 1967 film Edipo Re.

JOCASTA A household slave, the only man to get back alive.

OEDIPUS And is he here now, still in the palace?

JOCASTA No. When he returned from there and saw
That you held power, with Laius dead and gone,
He begged me as a suppliant, his hand on mine,   760
To send him to the country to pasture sheep,
Out of sight of this city, as far as possible.
I sent him; he deserved, as a loyal slave,
To win this favour – and indeed much more.

OEDIPUS Could we get him back here again – and quickly?   765

JOCASTA We could. But what's your aim in asking this?

OEDIPUS My lady, I fear that I have already said
Too much by far. That's why I wish to see him.

JOCASTA Then he will come. But I think that I deserve
To understand what's troubling you, my lord.   770

OEDIPUS I'll not deny you; my anxieties
Have grown so great. Whom should I rather tell
Than you, when this is happening to me?
My father, then, was Polybus of Corinth;
My mother, Merope, a Dorian. I was regarded   775
As the greatest of the citizens there until
Something chanced to happen that was strange,
Though it did not deserve the heat of my response.
At dinner, a man who was overfull with wine
Drunkenly claimed I was not my father's son.   780
Angry though I was, for that one day
I held back, though it was hard. But the next day I went
To my mother and father and questioned them. They were furious
At the insult and at the man who had let it fly.
I was pleased by their response, but even so   785
The insult rankled – for the word had spread.
So without my mother and father knowing, I went
To Delphi; as to my reason for going, Phoebus
Sent me away disappointed, but to my distress
He revealed another message, grim and terrible: 790

The third oracle (791–3)

At this point, halfway through the play, we are told the prophecy of patricide and incest for which Oedipus' story was famous (see *Background to the story*, pages v–vi).

● How do Oedipus' words (790–7) emphasise the horror of his predicted fate?

The murder

Oedipus' narrative of the murder in 800–13 is vivid; the correspondence in detail between Jocasta's and Oedipus' accounts seems to leave little doubt as to the identity of the victim, though Oedipus still withholds final judgement. In many societies there is a difference in law between types of homicide (the killing of one person by another): in English law, for example, 'manslaughter' is unpremeditated killing, whereas 'murder' is premeditated.

● Was Oedipus guilty of 'manslaughter' or 'murder'? Is there an element of self-justification in his account?

● Does Oedipus' behaviour here seem consistent with his character in the rest of the play? (See in particular **Oedipus' anger** page 26.)

Pasolini's *Edipo Re*

A film version of Sophocles' *Oedipus Tyrannus* was directed by Pier Paolo Pasolini in 1967 (see picture on page 56 and **Dreams** page 72). There are many differences between it and Sophocles' play, the most important being that the storyline is linear, beginning in a modern setting with Oedipus' birth; the early part of the film contains minimal dialogue and the killing of Laius (like the consultation of the oracle) is enacted, rather than narrated by Oedipus, in a barren landscape with alien costumes and weapons.

● Consider the differences for an audience between seeing a scene like this murder acted out, and hearing it related by one of the characters involved.

813–14 Now if this stranger/Has any family tie at all with Laius
The suspense becomes intense as Oedipus comes so close to realising part of his crime.

816 hated by the gods Towards the end of his speech Oedipus refers increasingly to divine forces at work (see 828 and 830; also 738). Here and at 828 the word translated as god(s) is *daimōn*, a word particularly associated with unpredictable supernatural powers to which one cannot put a name.

I must mate with my mother, and show to all the world
A progeny it could not bear to see;
I would also murder the father who gave me life.
On hearing this, I fled the land of Corinth,
From then on judging its position by the stars,   795
To a place where I might never see the disgrace
Of those evil oracles concerning me fulfilled.
And as I travelled, I came to this very region
In which you say the king here met his death.
My lady, I will tell you the truth. As I made my way   800
And came close to the place where the three roads met,
It was there that a herald, and a man who rode
In a horse-drawn carriage, just as you describe,
Met me; and the one in front and the old man too
Violently tried to thrust me from the road.   805
The one who pushed me aside, the carriage driver,
I struck in anger; and the old man, when he saw this,
Watched for me as I passed the carriage, then brought
His double goad down on the middle of my head.
He paid a heavier price for this, for quickly   810
I hit him with the staff in my hand, and he rolled
Right out of the carriage, flat upon his back.
I killed them, every one. Now if this stranger
Has any family tie at all with Laius,
Who could there be more wretched now than me,   815
Who could be more hated by the gods?

819–20 and no one else/Imposed this curse upon me but myself!
Oedipus' perception of this irony comes late but, for the audience
watching him, it is no less disturbing for that. Oedipus still does not
understand the full implications of the pollution or of his own
uncleanness (823). This idea of defilement is also conveyed by
Oedipus' word 'stained' (833), often used of blood, but also used
metaphorically, as we speak of a stain on someone's reputation (see
also **Pollution** page 10).

824–5 my own people … my native land Oedipus, of course, speaks
of Polybus and Merope, and of Corinth (774–5, 794).

826 yoked in marriage Agricultural metaphors are common in
describing marriage and the procreation of children (see also 1404–5,
1497). This image here emphasises the seemingly inexorable nature of
Oedipus' destiny: the bull has no choice over whether to wear the
yoke, or as to who his yoke-mate is; he cannot escape the yoke until it
is removed for him.

827 Polybus who gave me nurture, gave me life The Greek uses two
strong verbs which emphasise a father's role and therefore the
enormity of patricide. Oedipus naturally, and in ignorance, speaks of
Polybus giving him both 'life' and 'nurture' (the order has been
reversed in translation).

830 you pure and reverend gods Oedipus ends his speech with a
prayer to the holy reverence of the gods (*theōn*) (compare 816). The
language here is devout and urgent (compare note on 216–18 and
Oedipus' prayer(s) page 22).
● For what is Oedipus praying?

No stranger now, nor any citizen
May receive me in his house or talk to me,
But must drive me from his home – and no one else
Imposed this curse upon me but myself!   820
And I defile the bed of the man I killed
With the hands that killed him. Am I not then evil?
Am I not utterly unclean? For I must be exiled,
And in exile I must not see my own people
Or set foot in my native land – unless I am to   825
Be yoked in marriage with my mother and kill my father
Polybus who gave me nurture, gave me life.
If someone judged that a cruel god had brought
These things upon me, would he not be right?
Never, never, you pure and reverend gods,   830
May I see this day, but may I rather vanish
Utterly from the world of men before
I see myself stained with such disaster.

CHORUS This frightens us, my lord. But until such time
As you learn the facts from the one who was there, be hopeful.   835

OEDIPUS Indeed, I have no other grounds for hope;
I must simply await the arrival of the shepherd.

*Laurence Olivier as Oedipus and Sybil Thorndike as Jocasta
in the Old Vic production, London, 1945.*

842 Robbers Oedipus recalls the piece of information he was given in the Prologue (122–3; see **One witness**, **one clue** page 12).

847 The scales tilt The image of scales as indicators of fate is found in the *Iliad* (*viii*, 69–70 and *xxii*, 209–10) (see also 961).
● How appropriate does this image seem here?

851–2 even if he departs from his previous account,/He will never show Jocasta's argument takes an odd turn: despite her statement at 848–50 she accepts that the witness might alter his story from that heard in 122–3, but her conclusion is not that Oedipus might still be innocent (or at least could not be *proved* guilty) of Laius' murder, rather that the murderer could not have been Laius' son and therefore that oracles are not to be trusted.
● How rational is Jocasta's defence of her husband at this critical moment? Is he her first concern?

Review of the Second Episode
Much has happened in the Second Episode to affect our views of the major characters (Creon, Oedipus and Jocasta).
● Has your response to each of the characters altered during the course of this scene?
○ Consider ways of representing the relationship between Oedipus and Jocasta on stage. How intimate is this scene? What effect(s) could be created by moments of physical contact?

SECOND CHORAL ODE (2ND *STASIMON*) (863–910)
This is a powerful and complex ode that comes at an important moment in the play. At one level it seems to look back at preceding events (see notes on 873, 894, 897–902; lines 906–9); but it also reflects generally on issues raised by the play and their significance for the contemporary audience (see, for example, notes on 879–80, 896).

The Chorus pray for purity and holiness in accordance with the everlasting laws of heaven. Such purity is implicitly contrasted with hubris, *violent or outrageous behaviour, which leads to its own destruction. They pray for the punishment of arrogant and ungodly behaviour; why worship the gods if those who show disrespect for religion are unpunished? Unchecked neglect of oracles, in particular, spells the death of religion.*

JOCASTA And once he is here, what do you want from him?

OEDIPUS I will explain. If his story is found

  To match yours, I'll have escaped disaster.   840

JOCASTA What was special that you heard me say?

OEDIPUS Robbers – you said that he reported robbers

  As having killed the king. Now if he still

  Speaks of them in the plural, then I didn't kill him;

  One man can never be the same as many.   845

  But if he clearly speaks of a single traveller,

  The scales tilt, and this deed must be mine.

JOCASTA Be sure that this was what he clearly stated;

  He cannot go back and reject this version now.

  The city heard this story, not I alone.   850

  And even if he departs from his previous account,

  He will never show, my lord, that the killing of Laius

  Properly fulfilled the oracle that Apollo gave:

  He said that he must die at the hands of my son.

  Yet it can never be that that poor boy   855

  Killed him; he himself had died long before.

  So when it comes to prophecy, from now on

  I'll use my own eyes, looking nowhere else.

OEDIPUS You are right. But even so, there is the shepherd:

  Don't neglect to send someone to fetch him.   860

JOCASTA I'll do so at once. Let us go into the house.

  There is nothing I would do against your wishes.

865 The laws What these holy laws prescribe is made clearer in the third stanza (883–96).

866 Sublime The Greek (*hypsipodes*) is one of several plays (also 878) on the word 'foot' (see **'Swollen-foot'** page 76 and **The riddle of the Sphinx** page 6). The literal meaning in 866 is 'high-footed'.

867 Olympus The home of the gods, often specifically the mountain in northern Greece, is here personified (see also 1088).

870 oblivion The existence of the 'laws' (865) is independent of man: they exist whether or not man remembers them.

872 The god within them (also 882) No god is specified until the tentative invocation to Zeus at the end of the ode (903).

873 *Hubris* is a Greek word used of violent or insolent behaviour that invites punishment. An element of excess is implicit in it – of going beyond a certain limit – an idea reinforced by 'Bloated' (874). The product of this excessive violence (or disregard for moderation) is, according to the Chorus, a tyrannical regime that will destroy itself.

873 breeds This image might bring to mind Laius' begetting of Oedipus; Laius' act of *hubris* in defying the gods by begetting or killing his own child (see **Jocasta's story** page 52) leads ultimately to the fall of both kings, father and son.

873 the tyrant The use of the word *tyrannos* (see note on 514) is clearly negative here, contrasting with its more neutral uses in the Second Episode (hence its translation as 'tyrant'). It seems to cast the words and actions of Oedipus in particular in a negative light. The Chorus have just heard that Oedipus may have become their ruler not through a benign act, but by murder. They have also seen him threaten Creon with death, and dissuaded him only with difficulty from acting on slender grounds of suspicion. However, the violence of the Chorus' language and their choice of imagery seem barely relevant to the scene we have just witnessed and inconsistent with their character and attitudes so far. Their reflections seem more generalised, in keeping with the multiple function of the chorus in many tragedies, as characters in the action, as commentators on matters relating to the play, and in providing interludes that may vary the register, tone or pace.

879–80 the wrestling/That is good for the city The Chorus contrast two types of political ambition: 'healthy' and 'bloated'. Political activity was encouraged in democratic Athens. The reference echoes ideas in lines 408–9 and 543–4, but is also of 'contemporary' relevance to fifth-century Athens.

CHORUS   May it be my destiny to show
                Reverent holiness in all my words
        And actions. The laws prescribed for these are   865
                Sublime, and were given their birth
                In the clear air of heaven, Olympus
                Their only father; they were not born
                Of mortal nature, like man,
                        Nor will oblivion ever   870
                        Lay them to sleep.
        The god within them is great and does not grow old.

                Hubris breeds the tyrant; *hubris*,
                Bloated with foolish possessions,
        Which are neither right nor good for it,   875
                Climbs to the top of the building, and
                Plunges inevitably to sheer destruction,
                        Then finds its feet
                        No use. But the wrestling
                That is good for the city – that I ask   880
                        The god never to dispel.
        I shall never cease to regard the god as my champion.

The Chorus. National Theatre production, London, 1996.

886 the shrines of the gods The Chorus are concerned about respect for the forms of religion as well as for the gods themselves (see 711–12).

894 The arrows of anger It is difficult not to be reminded of the anger of Oedipus, so much in evidence in the last two episodes, though anger here could equally mean anger from the gods.

896 Why should I go on dancing? This is a brilliant and shocking line. Not only do we seem to hear the citizens of Thebes threatening to stop taking part in sacred dances, we are also confronted with an Athenian tragic chorus apparently questioning the value of the event in which they are participating: the original Chorus, whose very name means 'dance', were taking part in an act of worship within the festival of Dionysus (see *Introduction to the Greek Theatre*, pages 113–16). By seeming to step out of the play, they draw the audience's attention to the contemporary nature of the issues involved (see note on 897–902). This sort of 'meta-theatrical' moment (where attention is self-consciously drawn to the fact that the play *is* a play) is frequently found in fifth-century Athenian comedy, but rarely in tragedy.

897–902 No more … Unless these prophecies prove true In response to the scepticism they view as sacrilegious, the Chorus seem to offer an ultimatum. The reference 'The old oracles about Laius are fading' (906) can only refer to the oracle mentioned by Jocasta and her reassurance that it went unfulfilled (see **Jocasta's scepticism** page 54). Scepticism about oracles was current in Sophocles' time (see note on 387).

900–1 Abae … Olympia There was an oracle of Apollo at Abae in Phocis (see map, page vii); Olympia was a centre of worship in the west of the Peloponnese, sacred in particular to Zeus and Hera.

910 Religion dies The Chorus, unlike Jocasta (see **Jocasta's scepticism** page 54), draw no distinction between respect for the gods and belief in oracles.

Review of the Second *Stasimon*
- Compare this ode with the *Parodos* and the First *Stasimon*. How consistent are the attitudes and character of the Chorus?
- How does this ode reflect upon the previous scene (513–862)? Consider in particular your impressions of Jocasta and Oedipus.
- What exactly do the Chorus seem to be praying for?
- Consider the sort of music and dance that would most closely capture the meaning of each of the four stanzas.

Yet if anyone makes his way,
Arrogant in his deeds and his words,
With no fear of Justice, and no   885
Respect for the shrines of the gods,
May an evil destiny seize him
To repay his ill-fated insolence –
If he makes unfair profit
And cannot refrain from unholy acts,   890
Touching the untouchable in his folly.
What man in such circumstances
Will ever manage to keep
The arrows of anger from his life?
If behaviour like this is honoured,   895
Why should I go on dancing?

No more will I go in reverence
To the sacred navel of the earth,
Nor to the temple at Abae   900
Or that at Olympia,
Unless these prophecies prove true,
For all men to point out.
Powerful Zeus, if you are rightly called this,
Lord of all, may this not escape you,
Nor your deathless, everlasting reign.   905
The old oracles about Laius are fading;
Men now discount them,
And nowhere is Apollo openly honoured.
Religion dies.   910

THIRD EPISODE (911–1085)

912 the shrines of the gods Jocasta returns from the palace with an attendant (see 945) after the last choral ode. Their arrival seems well timed: she visits the shrines (see **Prologue** page 2) and makes offerings to the gods just as the Chorus lament the death of religion.

● Does this represent a change of view on Jocasta's part?

915–16 He does not judge/Fresh events by past ones Oedipus is made to seem confused and credulous, unlike the confident rationalist of line 398.

918 my own advice

○ Can we guess what this would be? Try improvising the scene within the palace that Jocasta has just described.

919 Lycean Apollo Apollo is referred to here by the title translated at line 203 as 'lord of light'. A statue of Lycean Apollo was sometimes placed in front of a house to catch the early rays of sun.

921 plague

● Do you think Jocasta is speaking literally or metaphorically here? (If literally, this is the last mention in the play of the plague afflicting Thebes.)

923 the helmsman of our ship (see notes on 56, 104, 420 and 422) The emphasis is now not on the troubles facing the ship, but on the fear of the pilot.

Coincidence?

Oedipus and Jocasta await the palace servant, and a new character arrives unannounced as Jocasta is praying to Apollo for deliverance. At a similar moment in Sophocles' *Electra*, while Clytaemnestra is also praying to Apollo, a messenger arrives. The timing of both arrivals seems coincidental, yet has great significance for the plot.

928 Here is his wife, the mother could also mean in Greek 'his wife and mother here' until one hears the end of the sentence (see **Dramatic irony** page 22).

937 It will naturally please you, but perhaps upset you too The Corinthian is happy to answer his own riddles (939; see also 961–3, 1018–20).

JOCASTA Lords of our land, the thought has come to me
    To visit the shrines of the gods, taking in my hands
    These wreathed branches and offerings of incense.
    Oedipus is overwrought; his mind is prey
    To every kind of anguish. He does not judge   915
    Fresh events by past ones, like a man of sense,
    But listens to anyone who talks of terrors.
    So, since my own advice is achieving nothing,
    I turn to you, Lycean Apollo – you are nearest –
    In supplication with these tokens of prayer: 920
    Give us deliverance from this plague and cleanse us.
    For now we are all afraid when we look at him
    And see his terror – the helmsman of our ship.
MESSENGER Could you tell me, friends, where I will find
    The palace of your ruler, Oedipus?   925
    Best of all, tell me his whereabouts, if you know.
CHORUS This is his house, friend, and the master is at home.
    Here is his wife, the mother of his children.
MESSENGER May she always be happy, and surrounded by
    Happiness, as the wedded wife of a man like him.   930
JOCASTA The same to you, my friend, for you deserve it
    For these kind words. But tell me why you are here:
    What do you want from us? What do you wish to tell us?
MESSENGER Good news for this house, and for your husband, lady.
JOCASTA What is this news? And who has sent you here?   935
MESSENGER The city of Corinth. As for the message I bring,
    It will naturally please you, but perhaps upset you too.

940 the Isthmian land Corinth is situated next to the thin strip of land (Isthmus) separating the Peloponnese from northern Greece (see map, page vii).

941 Isn't old Polybus still in power? Jocasta's questions, like those of Oedipus, are swift and to the point.

Jocasta's triumph

Jocasta's views about the fallibility of oracles seem to be vindicated: this is her second 'proof' (see 720–2).

● Has Jocasta always disbelieved in oracles?

949 Chance (see note on 977)

960 treachery … ? Oedipus' question brings to mind his earlier concerns (see also note on 965–6).

961 a small tilt of the scales A second reminder of how delicately balanced human life is (see also note on 847).

965 the shrine of the Pythian seer refers to Apollo's sanctuary at Delphi.

965–6 the birds/That scream overhead Oedipus has expressed scepticism before about this type of prophecy (see note on 311 and lines 396 and 398).

970 in that sense he could have died because of me Greek oracles were sometimes open to very broad interpretation: Herodotus tells how Hippias had a prophetic dream that he would sleep with his mother; this was fulfilled not by any act of incest, but by Hippias losing a tooth on Attic soil (his 'motherland') (Herodotus *Histories vi,* ch. 107). Oedipus makes a joke here about the notorious ambiguity of oracles, but line 972 shows his conviction – and relief – that Jocasta is in fact right.

● Should Jocasta's argument, if true, free Oedipus of all his fears?

JOCASTA What is it – and how can it have this twofold power?

MESSENGER The population there will make him king
    Of the Isthmian land. That was the local talk.   940

JOCASTA What's that? Isn't old Polybus still in power?

MESSENGER Not so, for death now holds him in his grave.

JOCASTA What are you saying? Is Oedipus' father dead?

MESSENGER If my words are not true, then I deserve to die.

JOCASTA Quick as you can, girl – go in to your master   945
    And tell him this news. Ah, oracles of the gods,
    Where are you now? This is the man that Oedipus
    Has so long avoided, fearing that he might kill him.
    Now he is dead – and Chance, not he, is the cause.

OEDIPUS Jocasta, dearest wife, what has happened?   950
    Why have you sent for me here, out of the house?

JOCASTA Listen to this man, and consider as you hear him
    Where the god's holy oracles now stand.

OEDIPUS Who is this man, and what does he have to say to me?

JOCASTA He is here from Corinth to tell you that your father   955
    Is no longer alive: Polybus is dead.

OEDIPUS What's that? My friend, give me the news yourself.

MESSENGER If what you want first is a clear report from me,
    Then here it is: that man is dead and gone.

OEDIPUS The result of treachery, or did illness come to him?   960

MESSENGER The old are laid to rest by a small tilt of the scales.

OEDIPUS So illness, it seems, was the cause of the poor man's death.

MESSENGER Yes, and the length of years he had measured out.

OEDIPUS So then! Why should anyone, wife, continue looking
    To the shrine of the Pythian seer, or to the birds   965
    That scream overhead? According to their authority
    I was to kill my own father; but he is dead
    And hidden below the earth. Yet here I am;
    I did not touch a weapon – unless longing for me
    Killed him: in that sense he could have died because of me.   970
    As for the oracles that faced me, Polybus has gathered them up
    And lies in Hades with them – they're not worth anything.

977 Chance (see also 442, 949, 1080) The alternative to a world guided by the gods who reveal man's fate through omens and prophecies is a random world of chance. Jocasta personifies Chance as if it were a god itself, but she does not necessarily deny the gods' power; she simply denies the possibility of man's knowing their intentions. Her philosophy is perhaps close to that of the fifth-century humanist philosopher Protagoras whose doctrine was that 'man is the measure of all things' and who expressed agnostic views: 'As to the gods, I have no means of knowing either that they exist or that they do not exist.' (trans. W.K.C. Guthrie) (see also note on 1409).

● Does this explanation account for Jocasta's words and actions at lines 911–23?

Dreams

Dreams were also credited by some with prophetic significance (see note on 970). Lines 981–2 have become famous because of the psychoanalyst, Sigmund Freud, who saw the influential production of *Oedipus Tyrannus* in Paris starring Mounet-Sully. In *The Interpretation of Dreams* (1900), he argues that the drama moves the modern reader not because it is a play of destiny, but because we recognise in ourselves the subconscious and primitive emotions represented in the Oedipus myth, particularly those directed towards parents. The phrase 'Oedipus complex', used to label a young male's (alleged) subconscious desire to kill the father and marry the mother, is a Freudian term.

○ How might a producer bring out the irony that it is Jocasta comforting Oedipus here? The picture on page 56 is a still from the film *Edipo Re* (see page 58); the director, Pasolini, has clearly been influenced by Freudian ideas.

986 I must feel fear Oedipus' conversion to Jocasta's philosophy is incomplete.

987 great relief The Greek uses a striking idiom, literally translated as 'a great eye', contributing to the numerous references to feet and eyes in the play (see note on 131 and **'Swollen-foot'** page 76).

991 What is it about her that makes you so afraid? The messenger's words remind us that what he has witnessed must be bewildering to someone who has not followed the drama so far. His innocent words and cheerful intentions bring a tension into the scene between the lightness of his responses and the deep concerns of Oedipus and Jocasta.

999 The greatest joy is to look into a parent's eyes The hard reality of Oedipus' self-imposed exile is set against his 'good luck' (998), but even Oedipus' simplest statements are not what they seem.

JOCASTA Did I not tell you long ago that this would be so?

OEDIPUS You did; but I was led astray by fear.

JOCASTA Well, don't take these things to heart any more.   975

OEDIPUS Yet my mother's bed – how can I not fear that?

JOCASTA Why should we humans fear, when it is Chance
    That rules, and there is no clear knowledge of the future?
    It's best, as far as one can, to live at random.
    You should not fear this marriage with your mother: 980
    In dreams, too, many men before now
    Have slept with their mother; but the man for whom
    This means nothing has the easiest life.

OEDIPUS All that you have said would be well spoken
    If my mother were not still living. But, as it is,   985
    She lives; and, however fine your words, I must feel fear.

JOCASTA Yet your father's burial should bring you great relief.

OEDIPUS Great, I know it; but I fear the living woman.

MESSENGER Who is the woman causing you this fear?

OEDIPUS Merope, old man, who lived with Polybus.   990

MESSENGER What is it about her that makes you so afraid?

OEDIPUS An oracle from the gods, my friend, a frightening one.

MESSENGER Can it be told? Or is it forbidden for others to know?

OEDIPUS It can be: once, Apollo said that I
    Must sleep with my own mother and that I   995
    Must shed my father's blood with my own hands.
    And that is why for so long I have lived
    Far from Corinth. I've had good luck, and yet
    The greatest joy is to look into a parent's eyes.

MESSENGER And was it this fear that exiled you from there?   1000

OEDIPUS Old man, I did not want to kill my father.

MESSENGER Then why, my lord, since I came with kind intentions,
    Do I not release you from this fear of yours?

1004–5 Be sure

- What is the effect here of the messenger's repetition of Oedipus' words?
- What effects are created by the *stichomythia* (line-for-line dialogue, see page 28) in lines 1007–15? Do you get the impression that the messenger is enjoying his side of the conversation?
- What sort of 'good' (1006) do you think the Corinthian has in mind?

1007 I will never go to the place where my parents are Later in the play Oedipus speaks of a meeting with his parents (1370–4).

1008 My boy

- How appropriate is the way the Corinthian messenger addresses Oedipus? (See also 1030.)

1012 Fear of catching pollution

- What does the Corinthian messenger's phrase suggest about his view of the oracle Oedipus has just told him about? (See **Pollution** page 10.)

1017 What's that you say? Oedipus' response to the Corinthian's news is a new sequence of questions which leads him closer and closer to understanding his full story.

- Is line 1016 the climax we expect it to be?
- Do you find Oedipus' response to the Corinthian's news psychologically convincing?

1019 How could my father be the same as a nobody? Oedipus' discourtesy doesn't stop the Corinthian once again from explaining his own riddle (see note on 937).

1023 Yet he came to love me so much? The love between Oedipus and his 'father' (see also 969–70 and 998) reinforces the impression of a secure and happy childhood.

1027 in this direction Corinth is the other side of Cithaeron (see note on 421) from Thebes (see map, page vii).

OEDIPUS Be sure that you would be well thanked by me.

MESSENGER Be sure that this was my main thought in coming
        here – 1005
    To do myself some good once you get home.

OEDIPUS I will never go to the place where my parents are.

MESSENGER My boy, it's quite clear you don't know what you're
        doing –

OEDIPUS What's that, old man? In the name of the gods, do tell me.

MESSENGER – if this is your reason for avoiding the journey home. 1010

OEDIPUS Yes, for fear that Apollo may prove to be true.

MESSENGER Fear of catching pollution from your parents?

OEDIPUS The very thing, old man – my constant fear.

MESSENGER Do you really not know? You've no just cause for fear.

OEDIPUS How could that be, if I am the child of these parents? 1015

MESSENGER Because Polybus was no relation of yours.

OEDIPUS What's that you say? Polybus was not my father?

MESSENGER No more than the man you see before you – about
        the same.

OEDIPUS How could my father be the same as a nobody?

MESSENGER He was not your father – and nor am I. 1020

OEDIPUS But why in that case did he call me his son?

MESSENGER You were a gift he received once from these very hands.

OEDIPUS From another's hand? Yet he came to love me so much?

MESSENGER He had no children before; that was his reason.

OEDIPUS When you gave me to him, had you bought me, or found
        me by chance? 1025

MESSENGER I found you on the wooded slopes of Cithaeron.

OEDIPUS Why were you journeying in this direction?

MESSENGER I was there in charge of flocks upon the mountain.

OEDIPUS You were a shepherd, travelling around for hire?

MESSENGER Yes, but your saviour too, my child, that day. 1030

OEDIPUS Was I in pain when you took me in your arms?

MESSENGER Your own ankles could bear witness to that.

OEDIPUS   Ah, why do you mention that old affliction?

1034 your ankles pinned together The coincidence with Jocasta's story (718) is all too evident.

1035 mark of shame
● For what reasons might Oedipus' ankles be considered a 'mark of shame' (see 1062)?

'Swollen-foot'
1036 your present name The Corinthian implies that Oedipus' name means 'Swollen-foot', derived from *oideo*, 'swell' and *pous*, 'foot' (and not therefore from *oida*, 'know', see notes on 58–9, 302). The irony of Oedipus' pun on his own name at 397 seems all the crueller: as well as not knowing who his parents were, did Oedipus not even 'know' the 'true' meaning of his own name? Word-play (see note on 417) continues to draw attention to Oedipus' name (for example 1038 'I (do not) know. The one who gave' is (*ouk*) *oid'ho dous* in Greek).

1050 Give me some sign; it is time for these things to be discovered Oedipus' questions intensify but he receives no answers at 1048 and 1049, and is forced once again to await the arrival of the first (118), and last, witness (1051–2; 756–69, 859–61).

The Corinthian messenger
The messenger remains on stage, silent, for the rest of the episode.
● What sort of character is the Corinthian? How would he dress and speak (but see also Fourth Episode, note on 1139)?

1059 Such clues Oedipus has been looking for clues since the beginning of the play (120, 221). In stories about abandoned babies clues are sometimes left with the child in the hope that it may one day be recognised: in Euripides' *Ion*, for example (see **Infant exposure** page 52), the word for such a clue is the same as that used at 221. Since in the case of Oedipus the hope was that he would *not* survive, no such clues were left with him. The word Sophocles uses here (*sēmeia*) can also mean a distinguishing physical mark, like Oedipus' ankles: one clue that has been literally 'at Oedipus' feet' or 'under his eyes' throughout (see note on 131).

1061 Stop this enquiry The enquiry prompted by Apollo in pursuit of which Oedipus vowed to 'make all clear' (132). Jocasta tries four times to stop Oedipus from asking further questions.
○ How could an actor make these appeals most persuasive? Do Jocasta's words suggest she varies her approach? How might Oedipus' responses affect her attempts to stop him?
● Is she speaking metaphorically when she says she is 'sick' (1061) (see also 60–1 and 921)?

MESSENGER I freed you; you had your ankles pinned together.

OEDIPUS A terrible mark of shame that I had from my cradle. 1035

MESSENGER And this mischance gave you your present name.

OEDIPUS Tell me, by the gods – my mother's doing, or my
     father's?

MESSENGER I do not know. The one who gave you to me knows
     better.

OEDIPUS Then you got me from someone else? You didn't find me
     yourself?

MESSENGER No. Another shepherd gave you to me. 1040

OEDIPUS Who was he? Do you know? Can you give me a clear
     description?

MESSENGER I think he was known as one of Laius' people.

OEDIPUS The king who ruled this country long ago?

MESSENGER Exactly. That's the man. And he was his herdsman.

OEDIPUS And is he still alive? Can I see him? 1045

MESSENGER You people who live here would know that best.

OEDIPUS Is there any of you standing near at hand
    Who knows the herdsman he is speaking of?
    Has anyone seen him here, or in the country?
    Give me some sign; it is time for these things to be discovered. 1050

CHORUS I think he is none other than the countryman
    You were keen to see before. But the queen –
    Jocasta here – would be best able to tell you.

OEDIPUS Wife, you know the man whom recently
    We desired to come here: is this the man he means? 1055

JOCASTA Why worry whom he meant? Think nothing of it.
    It's idle talk; forget you ever heard it.

OEDIPUS Impossible – when I have found
    Such clues as these, not to reveal my birth.

JOCASTA In the name of the gods, if you've any concern for your
    own life, 1060
    Stop this enquiry. Enough that I am sick.

1062 Even if I am revealed a slave Oedipus once again comes to a hasty conclusion (see **Oedipus' anger** page 26, **Oedipus' accusation against Tiresias** page 30; line 807) – and misunderstands Jocasta's distress, believing that she is concerned he may prove to be of servile birth. His anger flares up again and deflects him from the truth.

1070 Leave this woman to enjoy her wealthy family
o How might Oedipus say this line? Is it more appropriate to Oedipus' character and present mood if spoken sadly, bitterly or with contempt?

1071 unhappy man! Her last word describing Oedipus, *dustēnos*, is the word she used to describe her unnamed child at 855 ('poor boy') (see Fourth *Stasimon*, 1186–1222).

1080 child of Fortune The Greek word for Fortune here is *Tychē*, the same as that for Luck/Chance (442, 949, 977). As the child rescued from death by a shepherd's gift (1022, 1040) Oedipus seems lucky to have survived; but whether his survival was genuinely a question of chance/luck, as it now seems to Oedipus, is crucial to this play.

1082–3 the moons … /Have marked my progress Oedipus' poetic image suggests that the only 'relation' to see him grow up was 'time', here characterised as the months.
● Why do you think Oedipus uses this sort of language about his birth (compare 1019, 1062)? What does Oedipus mean by 'This is my nature' (1084)?
o How would you describe Oedipus at the end of this scene? The following words may help: *proud, defiant, stubborn, arrogant, noble, pitiable, humble, triumphant, selfish, lonely, powerful, brave, optimistic, frightened*.

Review of the Third Episode
● Trace the changes in emotional atmosphere during the course of this episode. How does Sophocles maintain the suspense?
● At what stage do you think Jocasta realises the truth?
o Consider the reactions of members of the Chorus to the revelations in this scene.

OEDIPUS Don't worry. Even if I am revealed a slave

    To the third generation, *your* lineage is sound.

JOCASTA Yet hear what I say, I beg you. Don't do this.

OEDIPUS I cannot do as you say, if it means not learning the truth.   1065

JOCASTA I know what I'm saying; I'm speaking for the best.

OEDIPUS This 'best' has long been irritating me.

JOCASTA Doomed man, may you never find out who you are.

OEDIPUS Will someone go and fetch that herdsman here?

    Leave this woman to enjoy her wealthy family.   1070

JOCASTA Oh, oh, you unhappy man! This is all

    That I can call you – nothing else, ever again.

CHORUS What wild grief, Oedipus, has sent your wife

    Rushing away like this? I fear that from

    Her silence some disaster will burst out.   1075

OEDIPUS Let it burst if it likes! For my part, I'm resolved

    To know my origin, however insignificant.

    She, perhaps, with all the pride of a woman,

    Is filled with shame at the thought of my low birth.

    But I consider myself the child of Fortune,   1080

    Who was generous to me; I will not be dishonoured.

    She is my mother; the moons, who are my kin,

    Have marked my progress – humble at first, then great.

    This is my nature, and I will never prove

    Different, to avoid learning my origin.   1085

THIRD CHORAL ODE (3RD *STASIMON*) (1086–1109)

The Chorus speculate about Oedipus' birth. They invoke Cithaeron, suggesting that association with Oedipus will bring the mountain honour, and call again upon Apollo. Was Oedipus the product of a sexual liaison between a god and a mountain nymph?

1086 If I am a prophet
- Does this opening to the ode seem playful or serious (see **Prophetic words** page 34, **Jocasta's scepticism** page 54)?

1088 Olympus (see note on 867)

1089 Cithaeron The Chorus capture the spirit of Oedipus' closing words by personifying the mountain where Oedipus was exposed as an infant. 'Fellow-countryman' (1091) is the first recognition that Oedipus is not in fact a stranger, but a Theban. The idea of the mountain as a mother is like that of 'mother earth' (see note on 970).
- How appropriate is the image of the mountain as a 'nurse'?
- Why do you think the Chorus call upon Apollo in 1096–7?

1098 Child, who, who gave you birth? The world of Greek mythology is populated by children of semi-divine origin, sometimes hidden to keep them safe from harm or recognition. The Chorus wonder whether Oedipus is the child of a liaison between a god (Pan, Apollo (Loxias, 1102), Hermes or Dionysus (see note on 209) – all of whom were associated with mountains) and a mountain nymph. Such a birth would be the antithesis of that of a slave (1035, 1077, 1168).

1100 Pan A god who was half-goat and half-man, Pan was known as 'Guardian of the Flocks' and, like his father Hermes (see 1104), associated particularly with Arcadia (see map, page vii). His own birth was the result of a liaison between Hermes and a nymph.

1102 Loxias Another name for Apollo.

1104 lord of Cyllene Cyllene was a mountain in Arcadia, the legendary birthplace of Hermes, son of Zeus and Maia. Hermes was the winged messenger of the gods and god of the boundaries between gods and men, life and death, indoors and outdoors.

Reversal of fortune (*peripeteia*)

Oedipus' anonymity raises him to new heights of good fortune in the wild speculations of the Chorus. In his analysis of tragic plots the fourth-century writer Aristotle identifies 'reversal of fortune' (*peripeteia*) as a common element; in tragedy this reversal is usually from prosperity to misfortune. Aristotle cites *Oedipus Tyrannus*, specifically the Third Episode, as a classic example (Aristotle, *Poetics*, ch. 6, 3; see also **Oedipus' appearance** page 94 and note on 1182).

CHORUS   If I am a prophet
And wise in understanding,
Then I swear by Olympus that you will know,
Cithaeron, by tomorrow's full moon
That you are exalted as Oedipus'   1090
Fellow-countryman, nurse, and mother;
And that you are honoured in dance by us
For the favour you bring
To our ruler.   1095
Healer Apollo, to you too
May these words bring pleasure.

Child, who, who gave you birth?
Which of the long-lived nymphs
Drew close to mountain-roaming Pan   1100
And made him a father? Did one who shared the bed
Of Loxias bear you? For he loves all the upland pastures.
Or was it the lord of Cyllene
Or the Bacchic god   1105
Who dwells on the mountain-tops
Who received you, a lucky find, from one
Of the dark-eyed nymphs, with whom
He loves to frolic.

Review of the Third *Stasimon*

- This *stasimon* has been called 'The only moment of sustained joy in the play' (Segal, *Oedipus Tyrannus*). Do you agree? What is the effect of such an emotion here?
- Are the Chorus suggesting that Oedipus might be a god?
- It is likely that Oedipus remains on stage for this ode since he is first to see the messenger when he arrives (1110–11). Consider the different effects of the Chorus addressing him directly ('Child' 1098) or of his sitting/standing apart.

FOURTH EPISODE (1110–85)

1111–12 the herdsman/Whom we have long been seeking (see 1040–52)

1116 You'll have the advantage over me Oedipus uses his powers of reason in identifying the man, but is still the stranger (220). The identity of this man is crucial and Oedipus is careful in establishing it.

1121 You there! Old man, look at me and answer
- What hints might this line give to an actor playing the old man about his behaviour so far?

Interrogation

Much of Oedipus' dialogue in the play has taken the form of questions; he has rejected Jocasta's plea to stop his enquiry (1061) because of his need to learn the truth (1058, 1065, 1076–7).

- How well chosen do you consider Oedipus' questions (1122–30)?
- How helpful are the herdsman's answers (1123–44)?
- What is the effect of the Corinthian messenger's interjection (1132–40)?

1137 the rising of Arcturus Arcturus is a star in the constellation Boötes. In September it appears as a bright morning star.

1139 my folds … Laius'
- Does this suggest a difference in the relative status of the two shepherds?

OEDIPUS Elders, though I have never met the man,　　　1110
　　　If I may guess, I think I can see the herdsman
　　　Whom we have long been seeking. In length of years
　　　He harmonises with this stranger here.
　　　Besides, those bringing him I recognise
　　　As my own servants. But as for knowing the man,　　　1115
　　　You'll have the advantage over me, if you have seen him before.
CHORUS I do recognise him, you may be sure. He was Laius'
　　　Herdsman, a loyal servant if ever there was one.
OEDIPUS First I ask you, our friend and guest from Corinth,
　　　Is this whom you mean?
MESSENGER　　　　　　　　Yes, the man you see before you.　1120
OEDIPUS You there! Old man, look at me and answer –
　　　Whatever I ask you. Were you once Laius' man?
SERVANT I was: a slave not bought but bred in his house.
OEDIPUS What work, what way of life was your concern?
SERVANT Most of my life I spent tending the flocks.　　　1125
OEDIPUS And in doing this, what were your principal haunts?
SERVANT Sometimes Cithaeron, sometimes the country nearby.
OEDIPUS Are you aware of having observed this man thereabouts?
SERVANT Observed him doing what? What man do you mean?
OEDIPUS This man here. Did you ever have dealings with him?　1130
SERVANT Not that I can say at once from memory.
MESSENGER No wonder, master. But though he doesn't recognise me,
　　　I'll give him a clear reminder. For I'm sure that he
　　　Is well aware of the time when on Cithaeron –
　　　He with his two flocks, I with just the one –　　　1135
　　　We were neighbours together for three whole seasons,
　　　Six months from spring to the rising of Arcturus.
　　　Then for the winter I would drive my sheep
　　　Back to my folds, and he would take his to Laius'.
　　　Am I telling this as it happened, or am I not?　　　1140

1148 Your words need punishment Oedipus grows increasingly violent in his threats (1152, 1154, 1166).

1153 don't torture an old man We are reminded of Oedipus' temper and threats of violence to Tiresias, though there he stops short of actual physical violence (402–3). In fifth-century Athens, a slave's testimony was valid only if given under torture.

○ Who should respond to Oedipus' command at 1154? Members of the Chorus or guards already on stage? What sort of guard would you think appropriate to Oedipus (heavily armed? ceremonial?)? For how much of the play should they have been on stage?

● Consider the similarities and differences between this encounter between Oedipus and an old man, and the scene with Tiresias (First Episode, 300–462).

1165 don't ask me more The herdsman's words, like those of Jocasta, indicate how close Oedipus is drawing to the end of his search. It seems that one more answer will reveal all.

● How many more questions does Oedipus in fact ask?
● Why does he not question the witness about the murder of Laius?

1173–6 The pace of dialogue intensifies as Oedipus' questions become briefer. These lines are split (see **Antilabē**, page 46).

Attic red-figure amphora by the Achilles Painter. Shepherd with the infant Oedipus.

SERVANT Your account is true – though it was long ago.

MESSENGER Well, tell me, now – you know you gave me a child
  Back then, for me to bring up as my own?

SERVANT What's this about? Why are you asking this?

MESSENGER Here is the man, my friend, who was that child. 1145

SERVANT To hell with you! Will you not hold your tongue?

OEDIPUS Ah no, old man, don't try to chide him;
  Your words need punishment more than any of his.

SERVANT O best of masters, how have I done wrong?

OEDIPUS By saying nothing of the child he is asking about. 1150

SERVANT He speaks without knowledge; he is wasting his time.

OEDIPUS If you won't talk willingly, I'll make you talk.

SERVANT No! In the name of the gods, don't torture an old man.

OEDIPUS Quickly, someone, twist his hands behind him.

SERVANT You poor man, why? What are you so keen to learn? 1155

OEDIPUS Did you give this man the child he asks about?

SERVANT I did. If only I had died that day.

OEDIPUS And so you will, unless you give me the right answer.

SERVANT My death is far more certain if I speak.

OEDIPUS This man, it seems, is determined to waste our time. 1160

SERVANT No I'm not; I said before that I gave him the child.

OEDIPUS Where did you get him? From home, or from someone else?

SERVANT I wouldn't have done this to my own child. Someone
  gave him to me.

OEDIPUS Who? Which of our citizens? And from what house?

SERVANT No, master! In the name of the gods, don't ask me more. 1165

OEDIPUS You're dead if I have to ask you this again.

SERVANT Well then, he was a child of the house of Laius.

OEDIPUS A slave? Or born a member of Laius' family?

SERVANT Ah, I am on the terrifying brink of saying.

OEDIPUS And I of hearing. Yet this must be heard. 1170

SERVANT It was his child; so he was called. But the woman inside,
  Your wife, could best tell you about these things.

OEDIPUS Did *she* give you the child?

SERVANT   She did, my lord.

OEDIPUS For what purpose?

SERVANT   For me to do away with him.

1178 act of pity The herdsman would not have hurt his child (see also 1163) and shows pity that Oedipus' parents lacked. The herdsman currently experiences fear (1169), as did Oedipus' parents (722, 1175).

● How different or similar are these types of fear?

1182 Oh, oh! Oedipus' cry (*iou, iou*) is the same as Jocasta's at 1071. There seems to be nothing left for Oedipus to know. This change from ignorance to knowledge is called *anagnōrisis* ('recognition') by Aristotle in his analysis of tragic plots (see **Reversal of fortune** page 80).

1183 Light Looking on light commonly meant being alive.

Review of the Fourth Episode

● Consider how Sophocles creates dramatic tension in this scene.
● The herdsman is only a retired palace servant, but knowledge gives him some power over his rulers. How does he use this? Why do you think Sophocles chose this character as Oedipus' final witness?
○ The Corinthian and herdsman have had shared experiences and perhaps similar backgrounds (1132–40; see note on 1139). How could actors bring out their *differences*?
○ What emotions should an actor try to convey in Oedipus' final lines?

FOURTH CHORAL ODE (4TH *STASIMON*) (1186–1222)

The Chorus reflect on the illusory qualities of man's happiness and the futility of mortal life. Even someone who appeared so pre-eminently successful as Oedipus has shown this by falling victim to terrible suffering. They wonder at the nature of Oedipus' crimes, particularly that of marrying his own mother; but they recognise that his guilt was not deliberate and express their feelings at his fall.

1186 Oh, generations of men The idea of the transience of human life goes back to Homer and the lyric poets.

● The Chorus imply more than just the ephemeral nature of human life in the opening lines of this ode. Does their pessimism seem justified?

1190 happiness In Herodotus' *Histories i*, Croesus, wealthy king of Sardis, questions the wise Athenian Solon about happiness. Solon's answer is paradoxical: no man can be called truly happy until he is dead. Croesus only understands his meaning (a man's happiness can only be judged when his life is *complete*) after he has lost his kingdom and is about to be burnt alive. Oedipus illustrates this idea: though to others, and even to himself, he may appear happy, his tragic misfortune has been with him since birth; there has been no change in the events of his life, merely in his understanding of them.

OEDIPUS The child's mother? How could she?

SERVANT   She feared an oracle.   1175

OEDIPUS Saying what?

SERVANT   Word had it that he would kill his parents.

OEDIPUS Then why did you let him go to this old man?

SERVANT As an act of pity, master. I thought that he would take him
   To another country, his own. But as it is,
   He saved him – for great disaster. If you are the man   1180
   He says you are, be sure, you were born ill-fated.

OEDIPUS Oh, oh! The whole truth has now come out.
   Light, may this be the last time I look at you,
   Since I am revealed as cursed in my birth, cursed
   In my marriage, and cursed in those whom I have killed.   1185

CHORUS   Oh, generations of men,
                      When I add you together,
                      You amount to nothing.
                      For who, who wins more
                              Of happiness   1190
                      Than the mere appearance,
                      An appearance that fades away?
                      With your example before me,
                              Your fate, yours, O
                      Wretched Oedipus, I reckon   1195
                      No mortal happy.

1196–7 You shot your arrow/Further than all Oedipus' achievements are greater than those of any other, making his fall correspondingly great. There is an uncomfortable echo of the image in the Second *Stasimon* ('Climbs to the top of the building' 876).

1200–1 you arose/… as a tower The image may recall the closing lines of the priest's speech: 'A walled town … is worth nothing/If it is empty' (56–7); but here Oedipus represents the fortifications themselves, not simply the ruler enjoying their protection and power.

1202 My king The Chorus do not use the word *tyrannos* (see note on 514), but *basileus*, which is more suggestive of hereditary kingship. Oedipus has been shown to be a native king of Thebes, natural heir to his father Laius.

1207 O famous Oedipus The ironic echo of line 8 is striking; through the infamy of his acts, Oedipus has won far greater 'fame' at the end of the play than at the start.

1208–11 haven … furrows … ploughed Sea-faring and ploughing imagery are brought together here in describing Oedipus' sexual union with his mother.
- What relevance has the second image of the silent furrows for the rest of the play?

1213 You did not will it, but all-seeing Time has found you out The unfairness of Oedipus' fate seems difficult to comprehend. In some versions of the Oedipus myth, Oedipus' suffering is part of a curse on the house: the son is made to pay for the misdeeds of the father (i.e. Laius' seduction of Pelops' son, see *Background to the story*, page v).
- Is any hint given in this play of a reason for Oedipus' fate (see also **Jocasta's story** page 52, note on 1246–7)?

1214 the marriage – no marriage Riddling language is all that is possible in trying to describe Oedipus' human relationships (see also 1250, 1256, 1485 etc.).

1221–2 thanks to you that I breathed anew/And rested my eyes in sleep The Chorus use emotional language in expressing their loyalty. The image of new breath and secure sleep is reminiscent of the First *Stasimon*, which expressed the Chorus' relief after their deliverance from the Sphinx (lines 506–12).

Review of the Fourth *Stasimon*
- What sort of a world-view does Oedipus' fate and the Chorus' representation of it suggest to you? Do their conclusions have any impact on the way people should live their lives?

You shot your arrow
Further than all, and became master
Of unrivalled happiness and prosperity –
Ah, Zeus! – when you destroyed
The maid with crooked claws,
The singer of oracles; you arose   1200
Against death as a tower for my country.
Since then you have been called
My king, and honoured
Highly, ruling
In mighty Thebes.

But now, whose story is more sad to hear?
Who has come more to dwell with pain   1205
And savage ruin, through a twist in his life?
O famous Oedipus,
You were content with
The same great haven
As child and father,
The same bedchamber.   1210
How ever, how ever could the furrows
Where your father ploughed, unhappy man,
Have endured you so long in silence?

You did not will it, but all-seeing Time has found you out,
Passing judgement on the marriage – no marriage –
In which the child and father have long been one.   1215
Oh, child of Laius,
If only, if only
I had never seen you.
My lamentation
Pours forth in a great cry
From my lips. Truth to tell,   1220
It was thanks to you that I breathed anew
And rested my eyes in sleep.

- Could the play have ended satisfactorily here?
- What might an audience unfamiliar with the plot expect to happen next (see 97–8, 100 and 1182–5)?

EXODOS (1223–1530)
Messenger speeches
The appearance of this second messenger, unlike that of the messenger from Corinth (see **Coincidence?** page 68) is motivated by the events of the drama. His news, unlike that of the Corinthian (934–40, 959) cannot be told in a few lines. Messenger speeches reveal action that has taken place elsewhere, usually so violent that it was not shown. There was no 'taboo' on viewing the results of such violence or on describing what happened. The messenger speech in a tragedy is often a literary *tour de force*.

1226 house of Labdacus The servant, like the Chorus, has known more than one royal master in the palace. Labdacus was Laius' father and – as has now been revealed – Oedipus' grandfather.

1227 the Ister … the Phasis are mighty rivers that run into the Black Sea from west (the Danube) and east. No amount of water could cleanse the impurity of this house (see also **Pollution** page 10).

1230 Deliberate, not unchosen The messenger's words (1229–31) are designed to engage the audience's attention (see 1237, note on 1331).

1235 Jocasta … is dead A reminder of Jocasta's sudden exit at 1072. In Euripides' *Phoenissae* (see **Sophoclean prologues** page 2) Jocasta remains alive after the discovery of Oedipus' crimes, later stabbing herself on the field of battle over the corpses of her sons.

1239 as far as I can still recall The messenger is unnecessarily modest. As will become apparent, his powers of recall need no apology.

1246–7 that one-time sowing of seed,/Which had caused his death Attention is drawn to the consequences of a single moment (see also 1256–7). In Aeschylus' version, Laius was warned by the Delphic oracle that he must die childless, but was overcome by momentary lust, leaving his son to face the consequences of his weakness (see **Jocasta's story** page 52 and *Background to the story* page v).

1249 on the bed In Pasolini's film (see **Pasolini's** *Edipo Re* page 58 and **Dreams** page 72), the bed becomes a powerful visual image.

1251 more than I know The illusion that the messenger witnessed the events is sustained; drama is also created when, as the messenger describes Jocasta's final moments, Oedipus bursts into the narrative.

1255 a sword
- Why does Oedipus ask for a sword?

1258 some god The word is *daimōn* (see 816, 1301, note on 1311).

MESSENGER Most highly honoured citizens of this land,
What acts you must hear of, what sights you must see; how great
A burden of grief you must shoulder, if you are true   1225
To your birth, and are still concerned for the house of Labdacus.
I think that neither the Ister nor the Phasis
Could wash and cleanse this house of all its evils –
Those it conceals, and those it will soon reveal,
Deliberate, not unchosen. Of all our pains,   1230
The ones that hurt the most are those that are self-inflicted.
CHORUS Those that we knew of before were enough: they were
Heavy with sorrow. What do you have to add to them?
MESSENGER The quickest part of my message to say and understand
Is this: Jocasta, our noble queen, is dead.   1235
CHORUS Unhappy woman! Tell us, what was the cause?
MESSENGER She killed herself. But you are spared the worst
Of what occurred: you were not there to see it.
And yet, as far as I can still recall,
You'll learn just how she suffered, the poor lady.   1240
When, in her frantic state, she made her way
In through the hall, she rushed directly to her bridal
Bed, tearing her hair with both her hands.
Once she was inside, she slammed the doors,
And called aloud to Laius – now long dead –   1245
As she recalled that one-time sowing of seed,
Which had caused his death and left her bearing children
To her own child – a misbegotten brood.
She wept on the bed where, luckless woman, she had born
Husband to husband, children to her child.   1250
How, after this, she died is more than I know.
Oedipus broke in, shouting, and because of him
It was not possible to see how her suffering ended;
We were staring at him as he paced around.
He came up to each of us, asking for a sword: 1255
Where could he find that wife – no wife – that mothering earth
In which both he and his children had been grown.
He was in a frenzy, and some god must have guided him,
For no man did, not one of us standing near.

broke in (1252), **hurled** (1261), **forced** (1262), **fell into** (1262), **tore** (1268), **struck** (1270) The verbs used to describe Oedipus' actions are violent. His entry into the room – 'and from their sockets/He forced the bulging bolts' (1261–2) – seems to prefigure his act of violence upon himself (1270, see **The blinding** below, though the Greek words for 'sockets' at 1261 and 1270 are not the same).

Jocasta's death
Jocasta also hangs herself in Homer's version of the Oedipus story (see *Background to the story* page v): 'But Epicaste, tormented by anguish, hanged herself with a long rope she made fast to the roof-beam overhead' (*Odyssey xi*, 278–9). (Compare note on 1235.)

The blinding
The story that Oedipus blinded himself is also found in Aeschylus' *Seven against Thebes*. In another, probably later, version of the story by Euripides, servants of Laius blind Oedipus.

1279 A dark shower, a hailstorm of soaking blood Lines 1278–9 may have been added later, perhaps by actors. The 'hailstorm' of blood is a violent image, but the 'dark shower' and 'soaking' of blood into the ground could also have positive connotations of sacrifice and fertility.
● What impressions do you feel are created by this image?

1281 A disastrous mixture for both man and wife The Greek also means 'for man and woman'; the word translated as 'mixture' can also mean 'mingling' and is often used of sexual union.

The messenger's speech
● Consider the effect of the messenger's precise use of detail. How has he kept the listener's attention focused throughout this long speech?
○ How 'cinematic' is Sophocles' writing? How far could a film director use Sophocles' 'script' to 're-create' shots/camera angles? Investigate how the film director Pasolini directs this scene in *Edipo Re* (see page 58; **Dreams** page 72).
● What signs are there in the speech that the messenger is a sympathetic reporter? What difference does this make?

1287–8 show/To all the people of Cadmus Sophocles makes a virtue of theatrical necessity: as at 93, Oedipus chooses not to keep within the palace, but to face his people.

1289 His mother's – The messenger breaks off without finishing (*aposiōpēsis*). This effect draws attention to the enormity of Oedipus' crime, for which there is no speakable description.

1293 sick (see notes on 921 and 1061)

With a terrible cry, as if someone was leading him on,   1260
He hurled himself at the doors, and from their sockets
He forced the bulging bolts and fell into the room.
And there we saw the woman, hanged by the neck,
Entwined in a woven noose of swaying cords.
When he saw her, with a terrible howl of misery,   1265
He loosened the hanging rope. When the poor woman
Lay on the ground, what came next was dreadful to see.
He tore from her clothes the brooches of beaten gold
With which she had been used to pin her dress,
And lifting them high, struck his eyeballs in their sockets,   1270
Shouting that they would never again see
Him or the evils he had suffered, or inflicted;
But would see in darkness now those they should never have seen,
Failing to recognise those he had longed to know.
This was his chant as, again and again and not just once,   1275
He attacked and stabbed his eyes; and all the while
His bleeding eyeballs spattered his chin,
[Releasing not slow drops of gore, but all at once
A dark shower, a hailstorm of soaking blood.]
This disaster has broken from both of them, not just him –   1280
A disastrous mixture for both man and wife.
Their old prosperity was, before all this,
Prosperity indeed – but now, today,
Lamentation, ruin, death, shame – all
The ills that can be named: not one is missing.   1285
CHORUS Is there any respite now in the poor man's sufferings?
MESSENGER He shouts for the doors to be unbarred, and for
     someone to show
To all the people of Cadmus his father's killer,
His mother's – I cannot speak the unholy word he uses –
Intending to cast himself out of this land, and not   1290
To stay in the palace, cursed by his own curse.
But he has no strength, and needs someone to guide
His steps; for he is sick beyond all bearing.

SECOND *KOMMOS* (1297–1366)

The Chorus first respond in lyric metre to the sight of Oedipus. Again (see First *Kommos* page 48), Oedipus sings in alternation with them.

o Experiment with different types of music behind these lines.

Oedipus' appearance

There are striking differences between Oedipus' final and first appearances: instead of a ruler terrifying all with his curse (276), he is the object of that curse (1291). Instead of guiding the city (33, 41–2), he needs a guide (1292); Tiresias' riddling words (372–3) are clear as Oedipus becomes the blind man supported by his stick (455–6).

o Consider effective ways of representing Oedipus' self-mutilation.

o When should Oedipus enter? What do the Chorus' words (1297–1306) suggest about their reaction to his appearance?

Pity and fear

The messenger introduced Oedipus with 'you are about to see a sight/To move your pity' (1295–6). Evoking strong emotion was a prime function of Greek poetry and performance. One sophist (see note on 1409) says of poetry: 'Into those who hear it comes fearful fright and tearful pity and mournful longing' (Gorgias trans. MacDowell). Aristotle in the *Poetics* says that experiencing pity and fear by watching a tragedy has a 'purifying' or 'cathartic' effect.

● Are the emotions roused in the Chorus and in the audience the same at this stage in the play?

1304 much I want to ask you Another reversal of roles?

1307 Ah, ah, how miserable I am Oedipus, like the Chorus at 1303, uses the same word for 'unhappy/miserable' (*dustēnos*) as Jocasta used of Oedipus, both as baby and as man (see note on 1071).

1311 Ah god Oedipus addresses a *daimōn* (see note on 816), the force that has guided him through life, and who has suddenly made a great leap that he is only now beginning to comprehend. (See also 1301.) The Chorus' description of where the *daimōn* has led Oedipus, 'To a dreadful place, not to be heard, nor seen' (1312), emphasises his isolation and their difficulty in comprehending his position.

1322 You are the only one left Oedipus' blindness leaves him disoriented (1309–10) and alone. The harsh wind and darkness (1313–15) contribute to this effect. Many of the central characters in Sophocles' extant plays are figures who are or become isolated.

● Has Oedipus seemed an isolated figure earlier in the play (see First *Stasimon*)?

But he will show you; look, the gates are being
Unbarred; you are about to see a sight   1295
To move your pity, even though you may hate it.

CHORUS   Suffering terrible for men to see,
                Suffering more terrible than I have ever
                Encountered. Unhappy man,
                What madness came upon you? Who   1300
                Was the god who outleapt all others
                To attend to your ungodly fate?
                Ah, ah unhappy man, I can no longer
          Look at you, though there's much I want to ask you,
                Much to find out, and much to draw my gaze.   1305
                How you make me shudder!
OEDIPUS   Ah, ah, how miserable I am,
          A wretched creature. Where on earth am I going?
          Where is my voice being carried, fluttering about?   1310
                Ah god, how far you flung me!
CHORUS To a dreadful place, not to be heard, nor seen.

OEDIPUS   Ah, darkness,
          Abhorrent cloud, unspeakable, attacking me,
          Inescapable, blown over me by a harsh wind –   1315
                         Ah!
          Ah, again! How they come upon me together,
          The stinging pain of these jabs and the memory of evil.
CHORUS No wonder, amid such sufferings as these
          That your sorrow and words of woe should be redoubled.   1320

OEDIPUS   Ah, friend,
          You are the only one left attending me, for still
          You wait with me, caring for a blind man.
                       Ah, ah,
          I can sense that you are there, I still recognise clearly,   1325
          Though I am in darkness, the sound of your voice.
CHORUS What you did was terrible; how could you bring yourself
          To mutilate your own eyes? What god drove you to it?

1328 Apollo (see 341) Oedipus replies with certainty that the *daimōn* responsible for his terrible suffering was Apollo. In some plays, particularly those by Euripides, when gods inflict suffering on mortals they outline their reasons and methods in the prologue (e.g. *Bacchae*, *Hippolytus*), though the punishment may seem disproportionate. Often a god appears at the end of the play (*deus ex māchinā*) to resolve the action of the play.

- If this play ended differently, with the appearance of Apollo *ex māchinā*, what might he say? How far would he accept responsibility?

1331 But the hand that struck them was mine Oedipus insists that his blinding was his own unprompted action.

- Why do you think Oedipus feels it important to distinguish between his own actions and those for which he holds Apollo responsible?
- What is the tone of this speech (1328–35)? What does it reveal of Oedipus' state of mind?

1346 No mortal more hated by the gods The contrast with the opening impression of Oedipus as someone favoured by the gods (38) is clear.

- Did Oedipus ever present himself as someone favoured by the gods?

1349 A curse on the man

- Would you expect the Corinthian messenger and herdsman still to be on stage? (In the original production, assuming only three actors (see *Introduction to the Greek Theatre* page 115), the actor playing the Corinthian messenger would have reappeared shortly as Creon.)

1355 dear ones (*philoi*) are the members of one's family and one's friends.

- Consider the implications of what Oedipus says in 1353–5: do his words make sense?

1366 This has been the fate of Oedipus

- How much understanding and self-knowledge does Oedipus display in the Second *Kommos* (pages 94–7)?

1367 I don't know The Chorus' words (*ouk oid'hopōs*) echo Oedipus' last word, his own name. Oedipus' retort to their suggestion that suicide would have been better than blinding shows their failure to understand his situation (see note on 1322; see also note on 1036).

OEDIPUS   Apollo, it was Apollo, my friends,

    Who brought to their conclusion these terrible, terrible

              Sufferings of mine.   1330

         But the hand that struck them was mine:

         No one but I ventured this agony.

           For why did I need to see,

        When nothing I saw could bring me joy?   1335

CHORUS It was exactly as you say.

OEDIPUS   What is there left for me to look at,

            To love, to greet,

        Or to hear with any pleasure, friends?

     Lead me away from this place, as soon as you can,   1340

     Lead me away, my friends – I embody destruction,

       There is none more cursed, and, what is more,   1345

         No mortal more hated by the gods.

CHORUS Wretched alike in your fate and your knowledge of it,

  How I wish that I had never known you.

OEDIPUS A curse on the man who took the cruel fetters

     From my feet in the upland pastures, snatched me   1350

         From death and saved me:

            He did me no favours

            For if I had died then,

        I should not have brought so much pain

         To my dear ones, and to myself.   1355

CHORUS I too could have wished this so.

OEDIPUS   I would not then have come and murdered

         My father, nor been called bridegroom

         Of the woman who gave me birth.

    Now I am shunned by the gods, child of unholy parents,   1360

    A wretch who shared my father's bed with my mother.

       If there is any evil more grave than another,   1365

         This has been the fate of Oedipus.

CHORUS I don't know if I can say you made the right decision.

  You would be better dead than alive – and blind.

Oedipus' defence?

Oedipus delivers a long speech beginning with a defence of his decision to blind himself rather than to commit suicide.

- Consider his arguments in 1369–85. How much sense do they make?
- What do you think of his idea that a human who could neither hear nor see could 'dwell cut off from evil' (1386–90)?
- Would you describe his arguments as predominantly rational or emotional?

1372 when I went to Hades Oedipus' argument requires him to remain blind even as a departed spirit, like Tiresias in Homer's underworld (*Odyssey x*, 493).

Apostrophē

In the second part of his speech (1391–1408) Oedipus retraces the story of his own birth, telling his story in the order in which it happened. There are many rhetorical devices in Oedipus' speech, almost as if he were pleading in a law court. One of the most striking examples is his use of *apostrophē*, where he addresses absent people and places he has known as if they were there before him. He calls on Cithaeron (1391), Polybus and Corinth (1394), and 'the place where three roads meet', which he describes in minute detail (1398–9). Finally, he speaks of events in Thebes (1402–8) and addresses the abstract concept of marriage, as if it were responsible for both his own birth and subsequent begetting of his children.

Oedipus blinded. Laurence Olivier in the Old Vic production, London, 1945.

OEDIPUS That what I have done was not done for the best

    Don't try to tell me; stop giving me advice.   1370

    For if I had sight, I do not know with what eyes

    I could have looked at my father when I went to Hades,

    Nor my poor mother, when against both of them

    I have committed deeds too bad for hanging.

    How could it be desirable for me   1375

    To see my children, born as they were born?

    My own eyes could never have wanted this.

    No, nor the city, nor its towers, nor the holy statues

    Of the gods: from these, utter wretch that I am,

    Though unmatched in breeding by any man in Thebes,   1380

    I banned myself, when I myself proclaimed

    That all should reject the sinner, the one whom the gods

    Have revealed as unholy – and as the son of Laius.

    When I myself had denounced this stain, my own,

    Was I then to look at these people with a steady gaze?   1385

    Never! Indeed, if there had been a way to block

    The source of hearing in my ears, I would not

    Have hesitated to imprison my wretched body,

    So as to be blind and to hear nothing at all.

    How sweet for the mind to dwell cut off from evil.   1390

    Oh, Cithaeron, why accept me? Why did you not

    Take me and kill me at once, so I would never

    Have shown mankind the truth about my birth?

    Polybus, Corinth, and the ancient home

    I called my father's, what a lovely thing you reared,   1395

    But with what evil festering beneath its skin!

    For now I am found to be evil, and evilly born.

    You three roads, with the well-hidden glen

    And oak-copse, where you narrowed at the junction:

1409 it's wrong The use of words implying moral and religious judgement intensifies in the play's closing stages: 'right' and 'wrong', 'pious' and 'impious', 'shameful'. There was increasing realisation in the fifth century that such terms could be conventional rather than absolute. Moral relativity is explored in the works of Herodotus, the tragedian Euripides and the Sophists, travelling professors like Protagoras (see note on 977) who taught rhetoric, politics and philosophy in fifth-century Athens.

● Does Oedipus' self-condemnation leave you feeling convinced that he is guilty of something essentially 'wrong'?

1411 hide me away … kill me, or cast me out With these orders, Oedipus embodies ruler and 'scapegoat' (Greek *pharmakos*): he is the source of pollution by whose expulsion alone the city can be purified. In Sophocles' day ritual driving-out of 'scapegoats', believed to take with them the troubles of the community, still took place.

1414 no need for fear
● What is it that the Chorus might fear? How reassuring are Oedipus' final words (1414–15)?
○ Should the Chorus respond to Oedipus' request to touch him before they notice the arrival of Creon? Or is it more effective if Creon's arrival leaves their response uncertain?

The arrival of Creon
Creon's status has changed. At lines 583–93 he talked about the merits and problems of kingship; here he appears as ruler in succession to Oedipus (see *Genealogical table* page viii; compare note on 1460).

1423–5 reproach … shame … respect Creon's words are self-consciously pious (1431). The Greek for 'piety' is *eusebeia* ('good-reverence') and his instructions show proper reverence to the elements (sun, earth, rain, light). 'Sun' and 'Light' have both been evoked at moments of great intensity in the play (661, 1183); for Apollo's identification with Light see 203 and note on 919.

● Do Creon's instructions to 'convey him into the house' come as a surprise?
○ Should his instructions be executed in performance?

Role reversal
Oedipus' and Creon's dialogue (1432–45) recalls some elements of their first exchange on Creon's return from Delphi (85–101).

○ Explore ways of emphasising the changes in the two men's situations.
● How consistent are the two men's characters in this pair of exchanges?

It was *my* blood, shed by my own hands, that you drank –   1400
My father's. Do you still remember me,
And the deeds you saw me do? And then, when I came here,
My further deeds? And oh, marriage, marriage,
You gave me birth, and after seeding me
Endured my seed in turn, and showed the world   1405
Fathers who are brothers and sons, incestuous blood,
And brides, already wives and mothers, and all
That men can do to reach the depths of shame.
But it's wrong to speak of acts that are wrong to do.
As soon as you can, in the name of the gods, take me   1410
And hide me away somewhere, or kill me, or cast me out
Into the sea, where you'll never again have to look at me.
Come, have the goodness to touch an unhappy man;
Do as I say – no need for fear. My troubles
Are such that no mortal can bear them except for me.   1415
CHORUS Here to meet your requests, just when you need him,
Is Creon: he will act for you and advise you.
Now, in your place, he is left sole guardian of our land.
OEDIPUS Ah, what words can I find to say to him?
What reasonable grounds for trusting me will he see?   1420
In my past dealings with him, I'm found to be wholly bad.
CREON I have not come to mock you, Oedipus,
Nor to reproach you with any past misdeeds.
You people, if you feel no shame any more
For the children of men, at least respect the all-nurturing   1425
Flame of our lord the sun: do not display
This object of pollution thus uncovered;
Neither earth, nor holy rain, nor light will welcome it.
Quick as you can, convey him into the house.
The family are the only ones who should see   1430
And hear the family's troubles: piety demands this.
OEDIPUS I beg you, since you've torn me from my fears,
Coming so nobly to such a worthless man,
Do as I ask – for your sake, not for mine.

1445 and now you too will believe the god
- What is Creon implying? Is this implied accusation fair?

Resolution

The play draws to a close with Oedipus giving instructions for the treatment of his family.

1447 her burial – the one in the house –
- Why do you think Oedipus refers to Jocasta in this way?

1451 Cithaeron This last reference to Cithaeron as Oedipus' tomb, combined with Oedipus' first accurate use of the phrase 'mother and father' in line 1452, is full of pathos.

Oedipus at Colonus

Sophocles' last play, written when he was nearly ninety, reverted to the Oedipus myth, taking up the story after the events in this play and those of *Antigone*. *Oedipus at Colonus* deals with Oedipus' mystic death in Colonus (a village near Athens from which Sophocles himself came); in the play there is rivalry between Thebes and Athens to provide Oedipus' last resting place. This tradition seems to be anticipated here (1455–7).

Oedipus' children

The audience has been made aware that Oedipus is a father since the First Episode (261; see also 425, 459, 1246–7 etc.) but no character has been given to these children beyond their incestuous begetting. Oedipus' thoughts naturally turn to them now.

1459 my sons Polynices and Eteocles are principal characters in the Theban cycle of myths (see *Background to the story* page v). After Oedipus' death they fight over who should rule Thebes and slay each other. Tragedies referring to these events include Aeschylus' *Seven against Thebes*, Sophocles' *Antigone* and Euripides' *Phoenissae*.

1460 they are men Creon's right to assume authority is undisputed within the terms of the play. Oedipus may mean that (as males) his sons are less dependent than his daughters or simply that they are old enough to stand up for themselves.

1462 poor, pitiable girls Oedipus' daughters, Antigone and Ismene, appear in Sophocles' *Antigone*. In contrast to Oedipus' brief words about his sons, full attention is given to the fates of his daughters.

Orphans

The fates of children after their parents can no longer protect them is an important theme in Classical Greek literature (see *Iliad xxii*, 490–5; *xxiv*, 726–38).

1465 they always had a portion themselves
- How does this domestic detail add to our understanding of Oedipus' character?

CREON What do you want? Why this urgent plea?   1435

OEDIPUS Throw me out of this land, as soon as you can,
  To where I can never be seen talking with human beings.

CREON Be sure, I would have done this, had I not
  First wanted to learn from the god what's to be done.

OEDIPUS His message has been made quite clear already: 1440
  Death for the polluted father-killer, for me!

CREON These were his words; but in our present need,
  Best to learn fully all that we must do.

OEDIPUS You'll ask these questions for a wretch like me?

CREON Yes, and now you too will believe the god.   1445

OEDIPUS Yes. Now I have a task for you. I beg you,
  Arrange her burial – the one in the house – as you wish:
  She is your kin, and you will do this properly.
  As for me, never allow my father's city
  To have me resident here while I am alive,   1450
  But let me dwell in the mountains, for Cithaeron there
  Is called my own, since my mother and father chose it,
  While they were alive, to be my appointed tomb.
  There they will have my death, where they tried to destroy me.
  And yet this much I know, that no disease   1455
  Or anything else can kill me. I would never
  Have been saved from death, unless for some strange doom.
  But let my destiny go wherever it will.
  Now for my children: as for my sons, Creon,
  Do not concern yourself with them: they are men,   1460
  And wherever they are, they will not lack means to live.
  But as for my poor, pitiable girls,
  Who never failed to share the food that was set
  At my own table, but whatever I
  Touched, they always had a portion themselves –   1465
  Please care for them and, more than that,
  Let me touch them with my hands and weep for their fate.

1468, 1471, 1475

- What effect do these three short lines, interrupting the regular rhythm, create?

Children on stage

Children appeared on stage in earlier tragedies (e.g. Sophocles' *Ajax* and Euripides' *Medea* and *Alcestis*). It is not clear when the children actually appear; it could be as early as Creon's entry at lines 1416–17.

○ Oedipus' blindness gives opportunity for visual dramatic irony (see page 22, 1472, 1480). What do you think is the most effective moment for the children to become visible on stage?

○ Consider the appearance and impact of the arrival of children on stage. How would they react to their father? In a production using masks, do you think the children should also be masked?

1476 I am the one Creon takes full credit for anticipating Oedipus' request. Like Oedipus earlier in the play (69, 287), he takes the initiative.

- Do you think his words make him appear smug or considerate?

1481 the hands of your own brother Oedipus demonstrates his full understanding of his history, now as teacher rather than student.

- Could the simplicity of his language (1481–5 and 1496–9) make these complex ideas comprehensible to young children?

1484 I saw nothing, I knew nothing The word for 'knew' here comes from the word for enquiry (*historia*, from which 'history' is derived). Oedipus explains to his daughters that he had no clues to help him understand what he was doing (see also 37–8 and 397).

Marriage

For a young woman to remain unmarried was considered an unenviable state: a woman's function was to produce legitimate heirs for her husband and see to the running of his household; he in turn provided protection and support. Without either a father or a husband, a woman's life would be marginalised and precarious. Oedipus' appeal to Creon not to let his daughters become 'husbandless beggars' (1506) transfers his authority and responsibility as *kurios* (male guardian) to Creon. In Sophocles' *Antigone*, however, Creon's own son, Haemon, is betrothed to Antigone.

Do so, my lord.
Do this, noble lord. If my arms could hold them,
I would think I had them still, just as when I could see.   1470
What is this?
In the name of the gods, can I not hear my own dear ones
Shedding tears? Has Creon pitied me
And sent my beloved children out to me?
Am I right?   1475
CREON You are. I am the one who has done this for you,
Knowing that it would please you now as it always has.
OEDIPUS You have my blessing. For bringing them here like this
May the god protect you better than he has protected me.
Children, where are you? Where? Come here, come   1480
To these hands of mine, the hands of your own brother,
By whose agency the once bright eyes of the father
Who gave you your being came to see like this.
But, children, I saw nothing, I knew nothing
When I became your father, though sown where you were sown.   1485
I weep for you both – I have no power to see you –
When I think of the bitter life that you'll have to lead –
That men will make you lead – from this time on.
What gatherings of citizens will you join?
What public feasts? You will come home from these   1490
In tears, rather than see the celebrations.
But when you reach the time for marrying,
Children, who'll run the risk or be man enough
To take the odium that will destroy
His family, just as much as the two of you?   1495
Is there any horror missing? Your father slew
His father, then sowed his seed in his own mother,
In whom *he* had been sown, and then got you
From the same source from which he had been born.
These are the insults you will suffer. Who then   1500
Will marry you? No one, children. It's perfectly clear
That you'll have to die barren and unmarried.

1515 You've shed enough tears now Sophocles uses a a new metre (*trochaics*) for this closing sequence (1515–30). Aeschylus similarly uses this metre at the end of the *Agamemnon*.

1520 I don't lightly say what I do not mean
● Has this been true of Creon throughout the play?

1522 No! Don't take them away Creon's reply suggests that the children are parted from their father.

Oedipus' exile?
There have been many indications during the course of the play which make the audience anticipate Oedipus' exile: the ruler's own edict (229, 241, 248), the prophetic utterances of Tiresias (420, 455–6), elements in the choral odes (467, 477–9) and Oedipus' increasingly insistent requests (1411, 1436, 1449–51, 1518, 1521); retrospective reading of Sophocles' *Oedipus at Colonus* also seems to justify this assumption. However, our expectations shifted at line 1429 when Creon instructed that Oedipus be taken into the palace and, although nothing explicit is said, the assumption is that Oedipus is led inside until the god has been consulted again.
● Death has often been mentioned alongside exile as potential punishment for the murderer (e.g. 100, 1411). Do you think Creon has this in mind in consulting the god?
○ Would the ending be more effective dramatically if Oedipus remained alone on stage? Why do you think the playwright chose to end his play in this ambiguous way?

The Chorus' final words
The Chorus' final words express ideas that were explored in other areas of Greek literature and which by the end of the fifth century were to become commonplace: that true happiness can only be judged once a man has reached the end of his life, since prosperity is always subject to changes in fortune (see note on 1190).
● Some suspect that lines 1524–30 were not part of the original play. Do you think the Chorus' closing words detract from or add to the effectiveness of the ending?

1527 wave of disaster The sea-faring imagery of earlier in the play is brought to its close here, with the helmsman's destruction.

Son of Menoeceus, since now you alone
Are left as their father, for we who gave them birth
Are finished, both of us, do not, as their father,   1505
See your own kin wander off as husbandless beggars;
Don't let them match the sufferings that I have,
But pity them; you can see how young they are:
But for you, they have lost all that they had.
Consent, noble sir, and touch me with your hand.   1510
For you, my children, if your minds were already mature,
I'd have much advice. But make this prayer for me now:
To live where opportunity allows,
And to find a better life than your father did.

CREON You've shed enough tears now. You must go inside the
    palace.   1515

OEDIPUS No pleasure in this; but I must obey.

CREON   All things in their season.

OEDIPUS You know my terms for going?

CREON   Tell me, and then I'll know.

OEDIPUS Send me to live away from this land.

CREON   Only the god can grant this.

OEDIPUS But the gods have come to hate me.

CREON   Then perhaps you'll get your wish.

OEDIPUS You're saying yes?

CREON   I don't lightly say what I do not mean.   1520

OEDIPUS Then take me away from here now.

CREON   Come, then – but leave the children.

OEDIPUS No! Don't take them away from me.

CREON   Don't try to take control.
    The power you gained before has not followed you throughout
    your life.

CHORUS Inhabitants of our native Thebes, behold here Oedipus.
    He knew the famous riddle, and was a most powerful man.   1525
    Which of our citizens did not look enviously upon his fortunes?
    But see now what a wave of disaster has overtaken him.
    So, being mortal, we should carefully look to the final day,
    And with that in view, we should call no one happy, until
    He has crossed the border of life without enduring pain.   1530

Synopsis of the play

PROLOGUE (1–150)

The scene is set before the royal palace in Thebes. Oedipus comes out to meet a deputation of citizens, led by an elderly priest. The city is gripped by plague and the citizens seek the king's help: he has saved them before from the tyranny of the Sphinx and has been acclaimed king because of this; let him show his power again. Oedipus replies that he has already acted: he has sent his brother-in-law Creon to Delphi to consult the oracle of Apollo. At this moment Creon is seen approaching. The message he brings is that the Thebans must get rid of that which is polluting their land – by either exile or repaying blood for blood. Creon explains that this must refer to the murderer of the previous king, Laius. Oedipus claims to know nothing of this, so Creon explains that Laius had been murdered while abroad; that the one surviving eyewitness had fled the city; and that preoccupation with the Sphinx had prevented a proper inquiry. Oedipus undertakes, for the sake of Apollo, the citizens, and his own personal security, to expose the murderer. The priest prays to Apollo for salvation and leads the deputation away.

PARODOS (151–215)

The Chorus enter – a group of Theban elders. They speculate about the meaning of the oracle and pray to the gods of Thebes for help. The land of Thebes is dying from the plague; they see Ares as the god responsible for it, and call on Athene, Apollo, Artemis and Dionysus to defeat him.

FIRST EPISODE (216–462)

Oedipus, who stresses that he is 'a stranger to this story, /A stranger to what was done' publicly demands that anyone knowing the identity of the murderer should speak: the criminal will suffer no more than exile. But anyone who knows and keeps silent will be banned from all further contact with his fellow Thebans. The Chorus assure him that they know nothing, but suggest that he consult the blind seer Tiresias, who 'sees/Much the same as lord Apollo'. Oedipus assures them that he has already sent for Tiresias, on Creon's suggestion. Tiresias enters, led by a boy, but refuses Oedipus' request to tell what he knows. Oedipus loses his temper and accuses Tiresias of collusion with Creon to unseat him as king. This in turn provokes Tiresias to accuse Oedipus not only of being the murderer whom he seeks but of living in an unholy relationship. Oedipus furiously dismisses Tiresias, who as he leaves taunts the king with a set of riddles to solve: who is the man who is both a stranger and a citizen, a sighted man who will be blind, brother to his sons, husband to his mother?

FIRST *STASIMON* (463–512)

The Chorus ask who can be the man meant by Apollo's oracle and imagine him as a refugee in the wilderness. The seer's words frighten but puzzle them: they accept that Zeus and Apollo know the truth, but find it hard to adjudicate between the wisdom of a human seer and the man who solved the Sphinx's riddle.

SECOND EPISODE (513–862)

Creon has heard of Oedipus' accusation and comes to defend himself. Oedipus, who has by now convinced himself that Creon and Tiresias are plotting to oust him, attacks Creon who attempts to show that, as the king's brother-in-law, he has influence without responsibility – for him an ideal combination. Oedipus is not persuaded and the wrangling continues until Jocasta emerges from the palace and stops it. She and the Chorus plead with Oedipus to accept Creon's word, and he reluctantly lets Creon go. Oedipus then tells Jocasta about the oracle and Tiresias' accusation that he is Laius' murderer. She tries to set his mind at rest by mentioning another oracle, given to Laius, which said that he would be killed by his own child: that clearly did not come true – the child was exposed on the mountain to die as a baby, and the sole surviving witness had reported that Laius was murdered by strangers at a place where three roads met. Oedipus' memory is triggered by the phrase 'a place where three roads meet' and he asks Jocasta for details: where and when was Laius killed? What did he look like? How was he attended? Jocasta's answers shock Oedipus and he tells her his own story. Brought up as the son of Polybus, king of Corinth, a chance taunt of bastardy led him to visit Delphi and ask Apollo about his parentage. Told by the oracle that he would kill his father and marry his mother, he fled, determined not to return to Corinth. On the road from Delphi to Thebes he met an old man, attended as Jocasta had described, was insulted, lost his temper and killed the lot of them. Is he then the murderer of Laius, and must he be exiled by his own proclamation? Jocasta insists that the oracle had said that Laius would be killed by his own son. Oedipus demands to see and interrogate the surviving witness to Laius' murder.

SECOND *STASIMON* (863–910)

The Chorus pray that in all their words and actions they may always revere the god-given laws. Immoderate behaviour leads to its own destruction; whereas they respect god and support healthy civic rivalry. Anyone who tramples on justice and religion deserves to suffer; if not, why honour the gods with dances? If oracles are proved false or are widely disbelieved, religion will die.

THIRD EPISODE (911–1085)

As Jocasta emerges from the palace with offerings to Apollo to avert the plague and to dispel fears about Oedipus' state of mind, a messenger arrives with news that Polybus is dead and that the people of Corinth want Oedipus as their king. Jocasta, taking this as proof that the oracle given to Oedipus was wrong, summons him to give him the news. He shares her joyous scepticism, but is still concerned about the part of the oracle relating to his mother. The messenger steps in to help: he can assure Oedipus that he was not the child of Polybus and Merope; the messenger himself, when he was a herdsman on Mount Cithaeron, accepted the baby Oedipus from another herdsman – a member of Laius' household. Oedipus asks if anyone knows of this man, and the Chorus suggest that it is the very person whom Oedipus has already asked to see. Jocasta will know … When Oedipus asks her, she tries to stop him from enquiring further, but he persists. With a cry that she hopes he never discovers who he is, Jocasta rushes back into the palace. Oedipus, assuming that she is afraid that he will be discovered to be low-born, imagines himself a 'child of Fortune', and insists on knowing the truth.

THIRD *STASIMON* (1086–1109)

The Chorus predict that Oedipus will be revealed as a native of Mount Cithaeron – and hence of Thebes; they hope Apollo will be pleased at this. They imagine Oedipus the son of some god or mountain nymph.

FOURTH EPISODE (1110–1185)

Servants of Oedipus enter, bringing the herdsman, who is recognised by the Chorus and by the messenger from Corinth. Oedipus interrogates the man, who admits to being a herdsman of Laius and to keeping his flocks on Mount Cithaeron. Asked if he recognises the messenger from Corinth, he is unsure, but when the messenger prompts his memory and mentions the child, he clams up until, threatened with violence by Oedipus, he admits that the child given by him to the Corinthian was Laius' own son, given to him by Jocasta with instructions to kill him. Why, asks Oedipus, did he not carry out his orders? Because he pitied the child. Oedipus, now certain of his ill-fated birth, rushes into the palace.

FOURTH *STASIMON* (1186–1222)

The Chorus reflect that, if someone as apparently fortunate as Oedipus can be so fated, man's life is nothing. He achieved more than anyone in defeating the Sphinx, and was highly honoured as king of Thebes, yet now he is ruined. They think with horror of the incest. Now time has revealed all and these citizens, once saved by Oedipus, wish that they had never seen him.

EXODOS (1223–1530)

A messenger emerges from the palace with the news that Jocasta is dead. After leaving Oedipus, she had rushed to her bedchamber and locked herself in, weeping as she invoked Laius and recalled the fatal birth that had led to her producing incestuous children. Oedipus had followed, frenzied and demanding a sword. He had burst into the bedchamber and found Jocasta hanged. After cutting her down, he had taken the brooches pinning her dress and had used them to blind himself. The messenger prepares the Chorus for his entrance and they ask Oedipus in horror what madness has led him to blind himself. In a lyric dialogue with the Chorus, he acknowledges Apollo as having brought things to their appointed conclusion but says that only he, Oedipus, is responsible for the self-blinding – because there was nothing that he could now bear to see. He wishes that he had died as a baby on Mount Cithaeron, and bitterly reviews all that he has now discovered about himself. Creon enters and Oedipus feels shame before him. Creon does not reproach him but insists that he must return to the palace and not pollute the daylight with his presence. Oedipus pleads for instant banishment, but Creon says that they must await further instructions from Apollo's oracle. Oedipus asks Creon to arrange Jocasta's funeral and to look after his children, especially his daughters. He hears them weeping and realises that Creon has brought them out to him. He blesses Creon and embraces the girls, lamenting with them and foreseeing that no one will now want to marry them. Creon gently but firmly puts an end to these lamentations, ordering Oedipus to let go of the children and to go back into the palace. The Chorus invite all citizens to look on the spectacle of Oedipus and to hesitate to call anyone happy until he has died a painless death.

Pronunciation of names

To attempt the authentic pronunciation of classical Greek names presents great difficulties. It is perhaps easiest to accept the conventional anglicised versions of the familiar names (e.g. Thebes, Zeus). The key below offers help with all the names in the play, which will give a reasonable overall consistency. Note that the main stress occurs on the italicised syllable.

KEY

ay – as in 'hay'   *ī* – as in 'die'
ē – as in 'hair'   *ō* – long 'o', as in 'go'

Abae	*A*-bī	Jocasta	Jo-*kas*-ta
Agenor	A-*gee*-nōr	Labdacus	*Lab*-da-kus
Amphitrite	Am-fi-*trī*-tee	Laius	*Lī*-us
Apollo	A-*pol*-lō	Loxias	*Lox*-i-as
Arcturus	Ark-*too*-rus	Lycean	*Lī*-see-an
Ares	*Air*-reez	Lycia	*Lī*-si-a
Artemis	*Ar*-te-mis	Menoeceus	Men-*oi*-kyus
Athene/	A-*thee*-nee/	Merope	*Me*-ro-pee
Athena	A-*thee*-na	Oedipus	*Ee*-di-pus
Bacchic	*Bak*-kik	Olympia	O-*lim*-pi-a
Bacchus	*Bak*-kus	Olympus	O-*lim*-pus
Cadmus	*Kad*-mus	Pan	Pan
Cithaeron	Ki-*thī*-rōn	Parnassus	Par-*na*-sus
Corinth	*Ko*-rinth	Phasis	*Fah*-sis
Creon	*Kre*-ōn	Phocis	*Fō*-kis
Cyllene	Kil-*lee*-nee	Phoebus	*Fee*-bus
Daulia	*Dow*-li-a	Polybus	*Po*-li-bus
Delian	*Dee*-li-an	Polydorus	Po-li-*dō*-rus
Delphi	*Del*-fi	Pythian	*Pi*-thi-an
Dorian	*Dō*-ri-an	Sphinx	Sfinks
Hades	*Hay*-deez	Thebes	Theebs
Ismenus	Is-*mee*-nus	Thracian	*Thray*-shun
Ister	*Is*-tēr	Tiresias	Tī-*re*-si-as
Isthmian	*Isth*-mi-an	Zeus	Zyoos

Introduction to the Greek Theatre

Theātron, the Greek word that gave us 'theatre' in English, meant both 'viewing place' and the assembled viewers. These ancient viewers (*theātai*) were in some ways very different from their modern counterparts. For a start, they were participants in a religious festival, and they went to watch plays only on certain days in the year, when shows were put on in honour of Dionysus. At Athens, where drama developed many of its most significant traditions, the main Dionysus festival, held in the spring, was one of the most important events in the city's calendar, attracting large numbers of citizens and visitors from elsewhere in the Greek world. It is not known for certain whether women attended; if any did, they were more likely to be visitors than the wives of Athenian citizens.

The festival was also a great sporting occasion. Performances designed to win the god's favour needed spectators to witness and share in the event, just as the athletic contests did at Olympia or Delphi, and one of the ways in which the spectators got involved was through competition. What they saw were three sets of three tragedies plus a satyr play, five separate comedies and as many as twenty song-and-dance performances called dithyrambs, put on in honour of Dionysus by choruses representing the different 'tribes' into which the citizen body was divided. There was a contest for each different event, with the dithyramb choruses divided into men's and boys' competitions, and a panel of judges determined the winners. The judges were appointed to act on behalf of the city; no doubt they took some notice of the way the audience responded on each occasion. Attendance at these events was on a large scale: we should be thinking of football crowds rather than typical theatre audiences in the modern world.

Like football matches, dramatic festivals were open-air occasions, and the performances were put on in daylight rather than with stage lighting in a darkened auditorium. The ideal performance space in these circumstances was a hollow hillside to seat spectators, with a flat area at the bottom (*orchēstra*) in which the chorusmen could spread out for their dancing and singing and which could be closed off by a stage-building (*skēnē*) acting simultaneously as backdrop, changing room and sounding board. Effective acoustics and good sight-lines were achieved by the kind of design represented in Fig. A on page 114, the theatre of Dionysus at Athens. The famous stone theatre at Epidaurus (Fig. B), built about 330 BC, and often taken as typical, has a circular *orchēstra*, but in the fifth century it was normal practice for

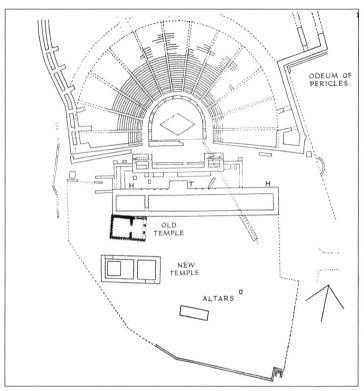

Fig. A. The theatre of Dionysus at Athens.

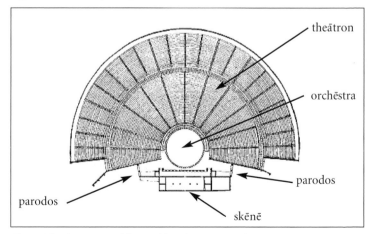

Fig. B. The theatre at Epidaurus (fourth century BC).

theatres to have a low wooden stage in front of the *skēnē*, for use by the actors, who also interacted with the chorus in the *orchēstra*.

Song and dance by choruses and the accompanying music of the piper were integral to all these types of performance and not just to the dithyramb. In tragedy there were 12 (later 15) chorusmen, in comedy 24, and in dithyramb 50; plays were often named after their chorus: Aeschylus' *Persians*, Euripides' *Bacchae* and Aristophanes' *Birds* are familiar examples. The rhythmic movements, groupings and singing of the chorus contributed crucially to the overall impact of each show, ensuring that there was always an animated stage picture even when only one or two actors were in view. The practice of keeping the number of speaking actors normally restricted to three, with doubling of roles by the same actor where necessary, looks odd at first sight, but it makes sense in the special circumstance of Greek theatrical performance. Two factors are particularly relevant: first the use of masks, which was probably felt to be fundamental to shows associated with the cult of Dionysus and which made it easy for an actor to take more than one part within a single play, and second the need to concentrate the audience's attention by keeping the number of possible speakers limited. In a large, open acting area some kind of focusing device is important if the spectators are always to be sure where to direct their gaze. The Greek plays that have survived, particularly the tragedies, are extremely economical in their design, with no sub-plots or complications in the action which audiences might find distracting or confusing. Acting style, too, seems to have relied on large gestures and avoidance of fussy detail; we know from the size of some of the surviving theatres that many spectators would be sitting too far away to catch small-scale gestures or stage business. Some plays make powerful use of props, like Ajax's sword, Philoctetes' bow, or the head of Pentheus in *Bacchae*, but all these are carefully chosen to be easily seen and interpreted.

Above all, actors seem to have depended on their highly trained voices in order to captivate audiences and stir their emotions. By the middle of the fifth century there was a prize for the best actor in the tragic competition, as well as for the playwright and the financial sponsor of the performance (*chorēgos*), and comedy followed suit a little later. What was most admired in the leading actors who were entitled to compete for this prize was the ability to play a series of different and very demanding parts in a single day and to be a brilliant singer as well as a compelling speaker of verse: many of the main parts involve solo songs or complex exchanges between actor and chorus. Overall, the best plays and performances must have offered audiences a great charge of energy and excitement: the chance to see a group of chorusmen dancing and singing in a sequence of different guises, as young maidens, old counsellors, ecstatic maenads, and exuberant satyrs; to watch scenes in which supernatural beings – gods, Furies, ghosts – come into contact with human beings; to listen to intense debates and hear the blood-curdling offstage cries that heralded the arrival of a messenger with an account of terrifying deeds within, and then to see the bodies brought out and witness the lamentations. Far more 'happened' in most plays than we can easily imagine from the bare text on the page; this must help to account for the continuing appeal of drama throughout antiquity and across the Greco-Roman world.

From the fourth century onwards dramatic festivals became popular wherever there were communities of Greek speakers, and other gods besides Dionysus were honoured with performances of plays. Actors, dancers and musicians organised themselves for professional touring – some of them achieved star status and earned huge fees – and famous old plays were revived as part of the repertoire. Some of the plays that had been first performed for Athenian citizens in the fifth century became classics for very different audiences – women as well as men, Latin speakers as well as Greeks – and took on new kinds of meaning in their new environment. But theatre was very far from being an antiquarian institution: new plays, new dramatic forms like mime and pantomime, changes in theatre design, staging, masks and costumes all demonstrate its continuing vitality in the Hellenistic and Roman periods. Nearly all the Greek plays that have survived into modern times are ones that had a long theatrical life in antiquity; this perhaps helps to explain why modern actors, directors and audiences have been able to rediscover their power.

For further reading: entries in *Oxford Classical Dictionary* (3rd edition) under 'theatre staging, Greek' and 'tragedy, Greek'; Simon Goldhill, *Reading Greek Tragedy*, Cambridge, 1986; J.R. Green, 'The theatre', Ch. 7 of *The Cambridge Ancient History, Plates to Volumes V and VI*, Cambridge, 1994; P.E. Easterling (ed.), *The Cambridge Companion to Greek Tragedy*, Cambridge, 1997; Richard Green and Eric Handley, *Images of the Greek Theatre*, London, 1995; Ian McAuslam and Peter Walcot (edd.), *Greek Tragedy*, Oxford, 1993; Rush Rehm, *Greek Tragic Theatre*, London and New York, 1992; Erich Segal (ed.) *Oxford Readings in Greek Tragedy*, Oxford, 1983; Oliver Taplin, *Greek Tragedy in Action*, London, 1978; David Wiles, *Tragedy in Athens*, Cambridge, 1997.

Pat Easterling

Time line

Dates of selected authors and extant works

12th century BC	**The Trojan war**	
8th century BC	**HOMER**	• *The Iliad* • *The Odyssey*
5th century BC 490–479 431–404	**The Persian wars** **The Peloponnesian wars**	
c. 525/4–456/5 472 456	**AESCHYLUS**	(In probable order.) • *Persians* • *Seven against Thebes* • *Suppliants* • ***Oresteia Trilogy:*** *Agamemnon, Choephoroi Eumenides* • *Prometheus Bound*
c. 496/5–406 409 401 (posthumous)	**SOPHOCLES**	(Undated plays are in alphabetical order.) • *Ajax* • *Oedipus Tyrannus* • *Antigone* • *Trachiniae* • *Electra* • *Philoctetes* • *Oedipus at Colonus*
c. 490/80–407/6 438 (1st production 455) 431 428 415 412 409 ?408 ?408–6	**EURIPIDES**	(In probable order.) • *Alcestis* • *Medea* • *Heracleidae* • *Hippolytus* • *Andromache* • *Hecuba* • *Suppliant Women* • *Electra* • *Trojan Women* • *Heracles* • *Iphigenia among the Taurians* • *Helen* • *Ion* • *Phoenissae* • *Orestes* • *Cyclops* (satyr-play) • *Bacchae* • *Iphigenia at Aulis*
460/50–*c.* 386 411 405	**ARISTOPHANES**	(Selected works.) • *Thesmophoriazusae* • *Lysistrata* • *Frogs*
4th century BC 384–322	**ARISTOTLE**	(Selected works.) • *The Art of Poetry*

Index

Bold numbers refer to pages. Other numbers are line references.

Euripides **2, 12, 90, 92, 96, 100, 102, 115, 117**
  Alcestis **104**
  Bacchae **96, 115**
  Hippolytus **96**
  Ion **52, 76**
  Medea *12, 104*
  Phoenissae **12, 90, 102**
exile **10, 20, 36, 50, 108**, 309, 418, 623, 641, 659, 670, 817–19, 1000 (*see also* Oedipus' exile)

feet **8, 14, 32, 52, 64, 72, 76**, 718, 1032, 1350
fortune (*see also* chance) **78, 106**
Freud **72**

gods **4**, 34, 38, 43, **54, 58, 60, 62, 64, 66–8, 82, 94, 96, 102**, 280, 815, 1009, 1060, 1258, 1346, 1439
Gorgias **94**

Hades **4**, 30, 177, 972
happiness, human **86, 106**, 1190, 1196, 1529
Hera **24, 66**
herdsman (*see* servant)
Hermes **80**, 1104
Herodotus **20, 70, 86, 100**
Hesiod **22**
Hippias **70**
Homer **v, 86, 117**
  The Iliad **16**
  The Odyssey **v, 24, 92**
hubris **62, 64**, 873

imagery **4, 6, 8, 12, 28, 32, 34, 38, 42, 52, 60, 64, 68, 72, 78, 88, 92, 106**
  agricultural **60**, 1211–12, 1246
  hunting **12, 28, 38, 42**, 542, 725
  sea-faring **12**, 23–4, **34, 52**, 56, **68, 106**, 422–3, 694–6, 1527
incest **v, vi, 58, 105**, 995, 1364
infant exposure **52, 76**
irony (*see also* dramatic irony) **14, 30**
Ismenus 21
Ister **90**, 1227

Jocasta **v, viii, 12, 22, 46–79, 82, 84–6, 90–2, 109–11**, 1446–7
Jocasta's religious views **54**
justice **22**, 274, 885

knowledge (*see also* understanding) **26, 30, 44, 52, 76, 96, 104**
kommos **48–53, 94–7**

Labdacus **v, viii**, 38, **90**, 225, 267, 495, 1226, 1245
Laius **v, viii, 12, 36, 88, 90, 108–11**, 1122, 1139, 1166–7
  death of **13, 20, 54–5, 58–9**, 139, 225, 308, 451, 558, 573, 852
  father of Oedipus **32, 90**, 814, 1216, 1383
  and oracles **52–3**, 906
  ruler of Thebes 103, 225, 759
law and legal language **14, 24, 26, 40, 58**
Loxias (*see* Apollo)
luck **34, 78**, 442 (*see also* chance, fortune)
Lycia 208

marriage **104**
masks **48, 104**
messenger speeches **90, 92, 116**
metaphor (*see* imagery)
metatheatre **66**
Merope **110**, 775, 990
metre **16, 24, 48, 94, 106**
miasma (*see* pollution)
moral relativity **100**
Moses **52**
music **18**

oaths **48**, 647, 653, 656
Oedipus' anger **4, 26, 28, 78**, 46, **50, 66, 78, 84, 92**, 337, 364, 405, 524, 674, 781, 807
Oedipus, character of **62, 74, 78, 100, 102**
Oedipus' children **102, 104, 105–7**
'Oedipus complex' **72**
Oedipus' curse **20, 38, 60, 96**, 276, 295, 351, 450
Oedipus' exile (*see also* exile) **101, 106**, 1436
Oedipus' ignorance **32, 76**, 398
Oedipus' isolation **38, 50, 94**
Oedipus as king **2, 6, 8, 14, 20, 32, 40, 88**, 628–9
Oedipus' name **2, 8, 30, 32, 76**, 1036, 1366
Oedipus' story **56**
Olympia 901
Olympus **vii, 64, 80**, 867, 1088
omens (*see* divination and omens)

oracles **8**, **10**, **12**, **16**, **38**, **52**, **58**, **66**, **70**, **74**, **90**, **109–11**, 149, 157, 604, 797, 853, 946, 953, 992, 1175
orchēstra **2**, **14**, **38**, **114**
Orestes **10**
orphans **102** (*see also* children)

Pan **80**, 1100
Paris **52**
Parnassus **8**, **38**, 475
parodos **16**, **18**, **114**
Pasolini's *Edipo Re* **58**, **72**, **90**, **92**
patricide **v**, **vi**, **36**, **58**, **60**, 793, 826, 967, 1001, 1357–8
Pelops **v**, **88**
Peloponnese **66**, **70**
Pericles **10**
peripeteia (*see* reversal of fortune)
Phasis **90**, 1227
Phoebus (*see* Apollo)
pity and fear **94**
place where three roads meet **54**, 730, 801, 1398–9
plague (*see also* blight) 28, **24**, **68**, 150, 921
pollution **10**, **60**, **74**, **90**, 96, **100**, **111**, 138, 242, 313, 353, 1012, 1427
Polybus **38**, **109–10**, 492, 774, 941, 971, 990, 1016–17, 1394
Polydorus **viii**, 268
Polynices **v**, **viii**, **102**
Poseidon **18**
power/authority **6**, **28**, **30**, **40**, 40, **42**, **50**, 236–7, 377, 380, 383, 534, 541, 586, 593
prayer **20**, **22**, 216, 239
priests **4**, **14**
prologue **2**, **24**
prophets and prophecy **24**, **26**, **30**, **34**, **70**, **72**, 310, 357, 398, 462, 709, 723, 747, 857, 1086
prophetic words (*see also* riddles, oracles) **34**, **80**, 791–3
Protagoras **72**, **100**
prothūmia ('readiness to act') **12**, **24**, **46**, 48
public and private speech **10**, **50**
Pythian (*see* Delphi)

questions **12**, **30**, **34**, **42**, **54**, **74**, **76**, **82**, **84**

recognition **86**
religion (*see* gods)
reversal of fortune **34**, **52**, **80**, 454

riddles **vi**, **6**, **34**, **36**, **68**, **88**, **108–9**
Romulus and Remus **52**

scales 847, 961
scapegoat **100**
scepticism **22**, **30**, **54**, **66**, **70**, **110**
seeing and knowing **8**, **26**, **30**
seeing and seeming **30**
servant (*see also* witness) **82–7**
sickness **8**, 60, **76**, **92**, 303, 1061, 1293
skēnē **2**, **10**, **40**, **50**, **114**
slavery **32**, **34**, **56**, **78**, **84**, 410, 763–4, 1062
Solon **86**
sophists (*see also* Protagoras) **94**, **100**
Sophocles **16**, **30**, **50**, **52**, **66**, **78**, **86**, **94**, **106**, **117**
  Antigone **30**, **50**, **102**, **104**
  Ajax **104**, **115**
  Electra **68**
  Oedipus at Colonus **40**, **102**, **106**
Sphinx **v**, **vi**, **2**, **5**, **6**, **12**, **34**, 36, **40**, **56**, **88**, **109**, **111**, 130, 391, 507
stage directions **10**, **20**, **36**, **82**, **84**, **92**, **94**, **96**, **104**, **106**
stichomythia **28**, **74**
supplication **2**, 41, 143, 327, 760
suspense **22**, **78**
'Swollen-foot' *see* feet

theatre, conventions of **10**
Thebes **v**, **vi**, **vii**, **108–9**, **111**, 152, 453, 1380
Thrace **18**
Thucydides **10**, **16**, **18**, **20**, **30**
time **34** (unity of place and time), 1213
Tiresias **v**, **24–38**, **42**, **50**, **52**, **106**, **108–9**, 705
truth **28**, **30**, **36**, **44**, 299, 370, 422, 500, 613, 1065, 1182, 1220
tychē (*see* chance, fortune)
tyrannos **40**, **64**, **88**

understanding, human (*see also* knowledge) **vi**, **8**, **30**, **34**, **38**, **40**, 43, **44**, **50**, **52**, 58, **96**, **104**, 395, 569, 677
unity of place and time **34**

wisdom 403, 436, 462, 503, 570, 692
witness/es **12**, **54**, **68**, **76**, 118, 755–6
word-play **4**, **8**, **30**, **32**, **64**, **76**, **96**

Zeus **4**, **16**, 18, **24**, **38**, **54**, **64**, **80**, 151, 158, 198, 497, 738, 903, 1198